a Framework for Learning

For adults with profound and complex learning difficulties

EDITED BY

CAROLINE ALLEN

Supported by PPP Healthcare Medical Trust

David Fulton Publishers

London

David Fulton Publishers Ltd
Ormond House, 26–27 Boswell Street, London WC1N 3JZ

www.fultonpublishers.co.uk

First Published in Great Britain by David Fulton Publishers 2001

British Library Cataloguing in Publication Data
A catalogue record for this book is available from the British Library

ISBN 1–85346–760–X

The publishers would like to thank Christine Avery for copyediting and Priscilla Sharland for proofreading this book.

Typeset by Mark Heslington, Scarborough, North Yorkshire
Printed in Great Britain by Bell and Bain Ltd, Glasgow

Contents

Foreword

I have been fortunate in being able to follow the development of Orchard Hill College of Further Education for several years, including the pleasure of a very illuminating visit to the college in its early days. That the years of work by the students and staff have been brought together in such a well-conceived book, to be make available to others working in the field, is very welcome. The information provided will benefit not only further education colleges, but also provision offered by social work and health departments. Indeed, it is to be hoped that schools, too, will draw on the material as there is much for them to learn.

Professor James Hogg
Director, White Top Research Unit
University of Dundee
November 2000

Acknowledgements

We would like to acknowledge the many learners, staff, colleagues, parents and carers who have contributed their talents and ideas to the development of this Framework for Learning over the years. We would like to thank Matthew Griffiths, Barbara McIntosh and David Fulton for their encouragement.

We are very grateful to the following people for giving us feedback on draft chapters: Heather Cole, Eve Clark, Thalia Crampton, Nik Crombie, Rasa Didzpetris, Nicola Edge, Alan Ellison, Michael Garcia, Mark Gray, Julia Hancock, Linda Howard, Michelle Humphreys, Peter Inglis, Penny Lacey, Gill Levy, Sid Lowe, Maria Marsh, Antony McCallum, Gail Petty, Maureen Ronksley, Sandra Saxton, Krisnaswamy Shumoogan, Jo Smith, Jane Townsend, Roseanne Tyas, Lorraine Walker, Sue Woolley.

We also thank Julia Stone for proofreading and feedback and the Orchard Hill College Administrative team for information gathering and administration. Thank you to Andy Linke at Creative Works for providing diagrams, and to David Murden and Nikki White for help with the index.

This book would not have been possible without the support of PPP Healthcare Medical Trust, the Orchard Hill College Governors and Officers from the London Borough of Sutton Learning for Life Group.

Introduction

A Framework for Learning describes the curriculum devised by staff and learners at Orchard Hill College during the past eight years.

During this time carers, parents, volunteers, advocates and professionals from many different disciplines have requested information about our work. This book is an attempt to share some of the most frequently requested information at its current developmental stage. The framework and accompanying practice is continuously under review by the team. To some extent the material presented here is another beginning for us, because it has made us look afresh at what we do and has given us an opportunity to gather reflections from others involved in similar work. We have attempted to make the framework for learning 'come alive' with a range of examples and case studies, although the challenge of striving to reflect the complexities of individual learner-led practice is one which we have found impossible to meet comprehensively within the book. The case studies reflect actual people and events, but the names of those involved have been changed.

The framework for learning was developed in recognition of the need for an overview to ensure that learners can experience a broad, balanced curriculum which incorporates choice, flexibility and the potential for individual specification, within a clear overall structure. The framework has grown from a strong learner focus. We did not devise a framework and courses and then fit learners into the structure. Instead, we developed and tested approaches, materials and structures over time. We created a framework that allows for the diversity and flexibility required by the range of individuals who have tested it and helped us, by their responses, to modify it.

This process is ongoing and represents the closest we have been able to get to achieving a framework devised jointly by learners with profound and complex learning difficulties and staff. Further comment relating to development of the framework and learner involvement is located in Chapter 1 and Chapter 2. The commitment to involving learners in 'having a say' is a theme which is developed throughout the book, in particular in sections on self-advocacy (Chapter 4) and choice (Chapter 7). It is recognised that the ethos of shared control, which is reflected in this commitment to a learner-led approach, must be apparent throughout daily practice. We have attempted to give examples of this throughout the book.

Eclectic approach

The framework for learning is flexible by design. It allows us to select whatever set of approaches work in practice with each individual and which enable each person to progress. Aspects relevant to the individual and the setting are extracted from approaches, rather than adhering to any rigid formula or any one model. The needs of many learners with profound and complex learning difficulties are such that approaches based on 'intensive interaction' or similar interactive models are often the starting point (refer to Chapter 3). Intensive interaction is based on the notion that 'if we could begin to establish a relationship with the students, and if we could establish a basis for communication, then all other spheres of teaching and learning would become easier and more meaningful' (Nind and Hewett 1994).

We have found that the framework is sufficiently open to absorb this and other interactive/experiential approaches, alongside a range of objective-led approaches which facilitate specific skill development. At the heart of all teaching and learning methods described in the framework is the acknowledgement that communication and relationship building between staff, learners and their peers provides the first key to ensuring that each learner experiences quality learning, whatever the context.

Information

- For information regarding interactive approaches refer to 'relationship building' in Chapter 3 and 'enabling learners to take the lead' in Chapter 10.
- For examples of objective-led approaches refer to 'objective setting' in Chapters 9 and 11.

The learners

The term 'profound and complex learning difficulties' has been adopted to describe the very varied group of individuals, many of whom are 'wheelchair users with high dependency for self-care, who communicate using a range of strategies (facial expression, signing, gesture, sound, touch) which may, or may not, include speech' (Orchard Hill College 1999).

Although the largest group of learners at the College function with profound learning difficulties, the College also provides courses for learners with more developed intellectual functioning (mild-severe) but who also have complex needs in relation to their autism, mental health issues, visual and/or hearing difficulties and communication difficulties manifested in 'challenging' behaviour.

Most examples and case studies within the book focus on learners with profound and complex learning difficulties. However, some examples of learners with complex needs but less profound intellectual difficulties have also been included to illustrate the high degree of flexibility inherent in the framework and, in some cases, to clarify some of the directions learning may take as progress is achieved.

Language

Having a background in education, we have opted for terms such as 'learning difficulties' in the book. There has been some effort to limit the use of jargon and words used only by certain professionals, because the book is intended to be used by all. Adult learners with profound and complex learning difficulties require support and 'teaching' from us all. Therefore, any language which might be considered to be specific to education should not be interpreted in any way as excluding people from outside the formal education system.

We have opted to describe the individuals we work with as 'learners', because the focus of the book is on enabling each person to learn and develop. Again, this does not mean to imply that it is only relevant in an educational context. Although some learning may be best suited to a college environment, many aspects of learning may be more appropriately placed in a range of contexts e.g. home, community facilities, work.

Understanding the layout of the framework

The framework includes the following:

* Aims   The aims and organisational features are outlined in Chapter 1.

- Foundation skills — The foundations skills, which are common to all study areas, are reviewed in Chapter 3 and some of the core subject chapters.

- Core subjects — The core subjects, shown in Figure 0.1, form the basis for Chapters 4–11.

- Additional studies — Additional studies focus on a specific aspect of a core subject. These have been mentioned briefly in relevant core subject chapters.

- Core subjects web — The interconnections between the elements of core subjects and the foundation skills are represented in a diagram of the web at the end of Chapter 3.

In addition to the chapters relating to core subjects and foundation skills, a further three chapters consider methods of establishing the framework and moving it forward. Chapter 2 continues the theme of learner involvement in creating and amending the framework. Chapter 1 outlines some organisational prerequisites for converting the framework into practice and Chapter 12 considers aspects of collaboration between individuals and services.

Each core subject chapter includes the core subject 'wheel'. The wheel diagram consists of labelled 'segments' which, in addition to the foundation skills, contain the key components of the core subject. Each chapter explores some of those key components through discussion, checklists and case studies. Subject chapters feature examples of: assessment, planning, learner choice and involvement, objective setting, teaching approaches, recording, reflection and evaluation.

Each core subject chapter has been written by the lead member of staff for that area. Although working to common aims and principles, often within common structures, each chapter reflects the unique approach developed from the experience of the learners and staff involved. While the framework offers a degree of continuity and a sense of security or 'knowing where we're going', its inherent flexibility allows for individual exploration and creativity, on the part of both learners and staff.

Choosing which parts to include and which not to include has been one of the most difficult aspects of attempting to represent the framework in book form. After all, the framework is a living, changing entity. It is not just a set of documentation,

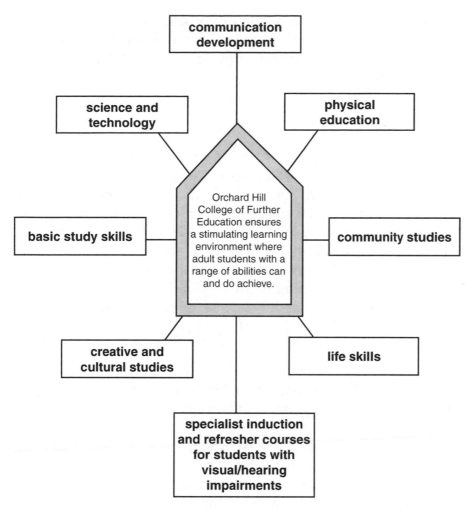

Figure 1 The core subjects

but an interaction between practice and its conceptualisation. The chapters which follow have been compiled to give a flavour of this process, but it is recognised that readers will need to extract and amend the content to suit each individual learner and each different work or home setting.

In many respects, the home setting may be an ideal learning ground. Communication is central to all aspects of learning and the daily routines of the home setting hold the potential to enable learners to develop communication skills in a familiar, comfortable environment. Other aspects of learning, such as self-care and household skills (refer to Chapter 7) may also be best suited to the home setting.

Learning at home

Learning for community living

Chapter 6 relates specifically to opportunities for learning in the community and other chapters feature case studies and examples which demonstrate ways in which learning may take place in varied contexts.

The potential of the framework

Chapter 1 and Chapter 12 explore some issues relating to potential uses of the framework for all sectors. Placing the learner at the centre, the notion that the framework could provide a 'common language' of practice for home and service providers is explored. It is mooted that the prospect of combined contributions of expertise, experience and different perspectives could be communicated through the framework. This could facilitate better quality overall for the individual and enable us to achieve greater clarity and cohesiveness.

Orchard Hill College

If you would like to share your ideas with us, or if you would like to visit the College to see the framework 'in action', please call us.

A 45 minute video of key aspects of our work is available for a small charge. Please contact the College for details. The College also runs practical workshop training sessions 'for practitioners by practitioners' at the College and other venues. Please contact the College for details.

Orchard Hill College of Further Education,
6 Elm Avenue, Fountain Drive,
Carshalton,
Surrey SM5 4NR
UK

Tel: 020 8770 8125/Fax: 020 8642 3763
Email: Orchard.Hill@ukgateway.net

Chapter 1

Creating the conditions required to put the framework into practice

The framework has been designed as a flexible structure which carries the potential to be responsive to the needs of every learner. It should be a dynamic entity which grows and changes as a result of a continuous quest to improve. In order to capitalise on this potential, it is critical that a commitment to responding to individual needs is at the centre of the organisation's culture and is reflected in all aspects of planning, decision making and operations.

We often seem to be subject to imposed restrictions and limited resources. Clarifying the purpose and direction of the service can help to ensure that we: a) remain learner centred, b) focus on what can be done and, c) have at our fingertips a sound rationale for the service which can be evidenced in practice.

Example

A visitor was introduced to our learners with profound and complex learning difficulties. He talked at length about his admiration for the staff, for their 'patience, dedication and skills'. Yes, the visitor was probably correct in many ways, but his comments rang alarm bells, as many visitors commenting in this way go on to express a view of our learners as 'unfortunates'.

My aim was for him to recognise that our learners were progressing, achieving, widening their horizons. I wanted him to see that the relationships between staff and learners reflected our strong commitment to recognising our learners as people with potential, people we respect.

I was able to influence the visitor's perspective by expressing clearly our principles and aims, pointing out ways in which these could be seen in practice.

Principles and aims

The first step is to compose the aims of the organisation, with everyone involved (Figure 1.1). The ideas should be generated by learners, staff and relevant others, rather than by the manager. There is a greater chance of genuine commitment to aims that have not been imposed, but have been carefully thought through and discussed.

Checklist for devising aims:

- involve everyone;
- express simply – avoid jargon;
- identify no more than six aims which are easy to remember;
- ensure that the focus on the individual learner is explicit;
- revisit aims regularly to ensure they are current.

Even if aims have been devised collaboratively, there is a risk that they may gather dust on a shelf. In order to be meaningful, the aims must be reflected in the everyday life of the organisation and referred to constantly, directly and indirectly.

Orchard Hill College of Further Education:

- provides an education service which offers equality of opportunity to all students and staff

- respects students as individuals and adult learners

- provides learning opportunities within a framework which is flexible and responsive to individual needs

- aims at all times to establish quality relationships and interactions which reflect the student's adult status and ability to learn

---

Figure 1.1   Example aims (Orchard Hill College 1999)

Examples for putting aims into practice

- Refer to aims when making and explaining decisions.
- Use aims to inform recruitment, induction and training.
- Refer to aims to identify an agreed 'concept of good practice' (Wyatt and Sherratt 1996) so that everyone knows how everyday actions relate to each aim.
- Monitor/appraise and support staff using aims as a point of reference.
- Revisit direct discussion of aims regularly.
- Display aims in every room and refer to them when planning and evaluating sessions.

See Figure 1.2.

In the process of creating a 'shared concept of good practice' learners, the staff team, governors, inspectors and relevant others gain an opportunity to reflect on what represents good practice. Once established, this 'shared concept' can be used as the basis for prioritising training, informing appraisal and evaluating the service.

There are some key elements to ensuring that the service is centred on each individual learner e.g. curriculum clarity and flexibility, enabling progress, learner motivation, incorporating

Aim	Shared Concept of Good Practice (examples)
Respects students as individuals and adult learners.	• Staff speak directly to the learner, not over his/her head. • Staff and learners explore together to discover mutual interests. Each learner is offered choices. Activity is negotiated, not imposed by staff. Staff creatively interweave learning challenges into negotiated activity. • Learning is planned with and for each individual learner, regardless of whether it takes place in a group or 1:1. • Activity is presented in adult style e.g. exploring water is carried out as experiments in Science and Technology, or as part of a swimming session, not as a water play primary school activity. • Learners are addressed as adults by using respectful body language, words and intonation.

Figure 1.2   Example of an aim translated into practice

learner's views, recognising achievements (Allen 2000). These key elements should be reflected in the organisation's aims and practice.

Reference to key elements can be found throughout the framework which is presented in the chapters which follow.

Some examples of key elements for the organisation include those listed in Figure 1.3.

Establishing agreement about organisational aims and practice in relation to these key areas involves confronting and working through attitudes and opinions, thoughts and feelings. This may be achieved initially through staff training opportunities and developed further through reflection and interaction between staff during daily evaluation sessions. The issues for debate might include attitudes to 'challenging' behaviours, equal opportunities, physical contact and age appropriateness.

Key element	Example management implication
• a focus on all forms of communication	Training in methods of communication given high priority.
• commitment to relationship building	Time and resource allocation (e.g. staffing levels) adjusted to allow for relationship building.
• recognition of the importance of enabling individuals to develop confidence and self-esteem	Formal recognition given to objectives relating to this area of development.
• flexibility to be able to respond to the needs and choices of each learner	Timetable constructed from consideration of each individual's requirement and choices, as opposed to offering ten places for each subject.
• a focus on enabling individual progress	Individual objectives monitored in relation to relevance to individual and opportunity for progression.
• commitment to incorporating learners' views	Evidence of adherence to learner choice making and responsiveness to learner 'comments' required as part of monitoring of service quality.
• recognition of achievement in all its forms	Awards for outstanding achievement include progress in all areas e.g. increased eye contact, greater level of participation with peers.

Figure 1.3   Examples of key elements

The framework has been developed specifically with adult learners in mind, although some parts of the work overlap the schools curriculum (for example, see reference to the National Curriculum in Chapter 8) in appropriately amended form. The concept of age appropriate learning is closely linked to the issues of respect for learners, the importance of forming relationships (refer to Chapter 3) and the requirements of learner-led development (refer to Chapter 2). There is emphasis on use of age appropriate equipment and materials, for example, use of real money not play money. However, this must not preclude the learner from keeping what is personally important to him or her. The notion of age appropriateness informs planning and resources, but this does not override the flexibility to respond to expressed choices from individual learners.

One of the key methods of communicating respect for learners is in relation to the spoken language, body language and actions of staff. The use of child orientated words of endearment e.g. 'poppet' or 'sweetie' are considered to be inappropriate, both in terms of age and in terms of a working relationship. Although many learners may require use of fairly

Age appropriate issues

Rachel's case

Rachel is a quiet person. She often hides away from people by pulling her clothes over her head. She has profound and complex learning difficulties, she has partial hearing, she uses a wheelchair. During one session, Rachel started to communicate differently with me. She reached out for me and seemed to be playing a game with me, hiding in her clothes and then appearing again with a smile. Her escort came to collect her that day from College. 'Don't suppose she did anything much,' the escort said (glancing briefly at Rachel). The escort was showing a lack of respect for Rachel, not only by her assumptions, but also by talking about her as if she was not there.

I answered the escort by saying, 'Actually, you were very involved today, weren't you Rachel? I liked the way you kept looking at me from behind your clothes. It was nice for me because it showed you wanted to communicate with me.' During this conversation, I looked and smiled at Rachel and the escort alternately in an attempt to make it clear that I was addressing both. I also used a tone of voice that reflected my respect and admiration for Rachel. (Aspects of good practice related to this issue are illustrated in Chapters 1, 3 and 11).

simple words, accompanied by other forms of communication, it is important that the tone of voice and body language used conveys genuine interest and respect. Attention to interaction between staff is also required to ensure that staff always include the learner in discussion, rather than talking over his/her head.

Touching is one further aspect of the age appropriate debate which has raised controversy in some areas. Most learners with profound and complex learning difficulties require physical contact to learn. Appropriate social contact is a key element of raising an individual's self-esteem; 'Touch can be affirming and supportive' (Sanderson *et al.* 1991). Clearly, safeguards are required to ensure that learners are secure from inappropriate physical contact, but sensible policy and practice should be the answer, not the type of restrictions which prevent the learner interacting with others by effectively banning touch. The framework incorporates a range of approaches which include appropriate contact (refer to Chapters 3, 9 and 11). Successful implementation of the framework requires clarity in relation to policy and practice. It is critical to ensure that this important form of communication is not outlawed through misinterpretation of the concept of age appropriateness or through lack of understanding on the part of managers and others in relation to the needs of learners with profound and complex learning difficulties.

Organisational culture

Johnson and Scholes (1997), suggest that organisational culture comprises three layers: *values*, *beliefs* and *paradigm* (taken-for-granted assumptions). The 'values' form mission statements and aims (see Figure 1.1); the 'beliefs' reflect commonly held notions about what is acceptable or not; the 'paradigm' includes aspects which people find difficult to identify and explain and 'exists in the minds and hearts of people within and around the organisation' (Johnson and Scholes 1997). The key is the paradigm which reflects the way the organisation actually operates. The 'shared concept of good practice', exemplified above, is an attempt to interact with the paradigm and interweave formal and informal dimensions.

The aim of providing a learner-centred service may be emphasised and reinforced through the formal monitoring process, but informal processes often also take a key role in ensuring sound practice at all levels of the organisation. Transferring good practice intentions into everyday actions requires attention to detail. It is 'the little things which count' and which communicate genuine respect and appreciation for each learner.

Examples

- Staff taking their cup of tea and sitting with a learner drinking theirs, rather than staff sitting together.
- Staff always speaking to the learner rather than over his/her head, i.e. instead of saying 'she did computer work', staff enable the learner to take part in the conversation. Example:

  Staff A: 'Hello Kay. What did you do today?' Staff B: 'You did some computer work today, didn't you Kay?' (Said while helping Kay to show a computer printout or object of reference.)

- Using age appropriate words and tone of voice.
- Offering and respecting choices.
- Using sensitive and appropriate touch when aiding the learner: the type of touch which communicates respect, liking and a sense that the learner and the task are the sole focus during the time it takes to complete the task.

Informally, such important details may be best reinforced by peer expectations. Staff working in teams can encourage each other to maintain appropriate standards, but this is only possible if they are given the support of managers whose everyday actions adhere to the organisation's agreed principles.

It would be meaningless to say to individual members of an organisation 'you must believe in x, y and z', but continuous dialogue about the language, anecdotes and practices can be used to influence values and create the 'paradigm', or shared assumptions, of the organisation.

Communication of the culture of an organisation begins at recruitment. Explicit reference to the organisation's aims and ways in which they are transferred into practice should form part of the first visit or interview. Discussions arising from

---

Example

A new member of staff continues to talk about learners inappropriately in spite of comments from the team. The manager is informed. The manager demonstrates her commitment to the organisation's principles by taking appropriate remedial action, training and supporting the new member of staff as well as supporting the rest of the team. The manager can be confident that her action is appropriate because the outcome benefits the learners and adheres to the organisation's aims and shared concept of good practice.

interview questions often provide an ideal first opportunity to discuss the organisation's shared concept of good practice and to provide the candidate with a chance to start to reflect on their own practice.

Some examples of interview questions:
- In this organisation, we work in staff teams. What skills do you think are needed to communicate effectively with colleagues?
- Many of our learners find verbal communication difficult. How could you help them to understand what you are saying?
- Our learners are adults. How would you reflect this in the way you communicate with them?
- How can you make sure that learners have a say in their own learning?
- Do you have experience of working with people with challenging behaviours? Why do you think people exhibit challenging behaviours?
- Have you read the equal opportunities policy? What do you understand it to mean? If a situation arises in which you consider a person to be in breach of the policy, what action will you take?

Consistently good practice i.e. highly learner centred with an emphasis on continuously striving to improve the service, requires regular discussion and staff training to facilitate evaluation and improvement of practice. This may take many forms, such as, 1:1 mentoring or 'support' meetings, formal training as a staff team or for an individual, discussions with carers and colleagues from other professions, recorded observation by a colleague of staff contact with learners, or role play during staff meetings.

Information

Guidance for training in relation to these issues may be found in: Collis, M. and Lacey, P. (1996) *Interactive Approaches to Teaching*. Griffiths, M. and Tennyson, C. (1997) *The Extended Curriculum*. Both are from London: David Fulton Publishers.

Learners with profound and complex difficulties often work with teams of staff in community homes, in colleges, day centres, employment bases etc. The team approach carries many advantages for creating the learner centred, high quality service recommended here. At their best, teams can capitalise on the strengths and talents of their members, gain strength from mutual support and reinforce and multiply the positive attributes of the organisation for the benefit of the learners. The strategies illustrated in this chapter are aimed at creating the prerequisites for teams to function at their best. One further strategy is the use of self/peer evaluation of staff performance. Working in teams has the potential to provide ideal circumstances for 'open' evaluation i.e. the type of evaluation which is perceived as non-threatening and as serving the 'common good' by directly benefitting learners and providing intrinsic rewards for the staff in helping the learners achieve (Figure 1.4).

Team approach

Evaluation Focus: facilitation of learner and learner interactions	
Strengths	Pacing was better this session. Sarah participated more fully because we gave her more time.
Weaknesses	We are giving too much hands-on support now, need to 'step back' and let learners take the initiative more. They're ready!
Next Session	Need to position Sarah and Jo closer together, they seemed to want to make contact. Try easing off hands-on support during hands-on interaction. Need extra time allowance for learner evaluation of session.

Figure 1.4   Example of evaluation form

If evaluation of the session/activity is made commonplace and regular, it becomes easier to incorporate improvements in staff performance. For example, it may be observed 'James (learner) became much more involved when Mark (staff) started to copy his vocalisations.' This evaluation comment can be used to reinforce effective teaching approaches and can benefit the learner directly by being highlighted as something to be followed up in the next session.

The curriculum framework provided in the chapters which follow, has been designed to accommodate the varied needs and choices of individual learners with profound and complex learning difficulties. Effective implementation of the curriculum framework requires a learner centred organisation in which there is synthesis between organisation level planning and operation and curriculum level planning and operation. The framework becomes a recipe for quality and success when it is implemented by an organisation with genuine commitment to the individual learner, a commitment which is evident and can be monitored. At this point, the framework takes on a life of its own and becomes a dynamic entity which evolves continuously in response to the changing needs and demands of its learners.

Example

The framework described in this book has grown over the years. One area which has been added is community studies (Chapter 6). Learners and their advocates were expressing a demand for more opportunities to learn and work within community facilities. The community studies subject area was devised in response to that demand.

Chapter 2

Involving learners in shaping the framework

'By sign, symbol, gesture, eye pointing or other means students can learn to choose between alternatives and to make their needs and wishes known'
(Sutcliffe 1990)

This chapter focuses on the ways in which learners with profound and complex learning difficulties can be involved in the process of steering their learning and shaping the framework. As in all areas of the framework, it is essential from the start to focus on establishing relationships and finding out about the learner's likes and dislikes (refer to the foundation skills in Chapter 3).

Ensuring the involvement of learners with profound and complex learning difficulties in the development and evaluation of learning is complex. These learners often have very limited experience of choice and involvement in decision making. Therefore, they require considerable support in order to participate. Many learners also experience difficulties in communicating their views in a way which can be readily understood by others. However, there is evidence to suggest that close observation and recording of learner responses may provide reliable indications of learner views (Hogg 1998).

Some ways of gaining learner involvement

- choice: the learner's preferences are acknowledged and are used to change or influence learning;
- evaluation: the learner's comments (verbal or otherwise) are acknowledged with respect and are used to influence planning for future sessions;
- leadership: the learner initiates new directions for learning.

Adrian's case

Adrian is a quiet, amicable man. He makes strong, beguiling eye contact with people when they position themselves at his eye level. He has profound and complex learning difficulties. He uses a wheelchair and has limited movement. Adrian has lived in a long-stay institution for most of his 30 years. When we first met, he seemed unaware of the concept of making choices. Staff worked closely with Adrian to find out his likes and dislikes and his methods of communicating. One of his 'likes' is water, so staff worked on offering Adrian a water activity e.g. footspa or watering plants and asking him to 'say' yes to the activity by taking his eyes to it. As Adrian progressed, staff introduced an alternative choice, so that whichever activity Adrian looked at with interest, the water activity or the other activity, this was taken to be his choice. Eventually, Adrian began to use clear eye pointing to gain his choice. Adrian is now learning to associate swimming with an object of reference (swimsuit and towel) in order to work towards making more abstract choices. (Refer to Chapter 4 for information about objects of reference).

Practice examples are shown in Figures 2.1, 2.2 and 2.3.

Choice

Learner comment	Outcome
Mary Mary enjoys a biscuit or snack with a drink. She chooses by eye pointing. 95% of the time, she chooses a chocolate something. When eating chocolate, Mary will usually smile and vocalise. She is far less enthusiastic when eating a plain digestive!	When setting up a tea tray, we always make sure there is a chocolate option for Mary. In this way, Mary guides our choice of resources.
Mohammed Mohammed uses a few words. He and I talked about which accredited module he would like best. I told him a couple of things which were in each module. As soon as I mentioned tidying away, which he loves doing, Mohammed said 'yes' and did a thumbs up.	Mohammed decided part of the course content.

Figure 2.1   Practice examples of learner choice

Evaluation

Learner comment	Outcome
Tom Every time we did a musical activity, Tom would be very alert, head up, smile, vocalise, wriggle about in his wheelchair. This sometimes happened for other activities, but not as consistently or as evidently.	We talked to Tom about our thoughts (i.e. that he seemed to really like music). We approached a music therapist and we are now doing a joint session with them every week for a term (this wasn't planned originally; Tom has changed the content and direction of the course).
James On an Information Technology course, James was always more tolerant of contact and more relaxed generally when on the mats (he was often quite tense when seated at a table and associated tables with food and drink).	James' 'comments' influenced where we worked with him. We began to take switches and other equipment to James on the mats and found that he was generally more motivated than when at the table.

Figure 2.2   Practice examples of learner evaluation

Leadership

Learner comment	Outcome
Patricia On an Interpersonal Skills course, Patricia showed leadership skills by arranging the seating plan for the group. She chose the order in which we sat down by looking at each person. She was able to choose people by eye pointing with increasing speed and accuracy, confirming the choice of who should sit down by vocalising.	Time was set aside to ensure that Patricia had an opportunity to lead part of the work.

Figure 2.3   Practice examples of learner leadership

The framework outlined in the chapters which follow includes examples of many different approaches to learning. Some approaches are clearly rooted in learning directed by the individual and their interactions e.g. intensive interaction (Nind and Hewett 1994), interactive massage (Sanderson *et al.*

Learner directed teaching approaches

13

1991), responsive environments (Ware 1996) and interactive approaches to teaching (Collis and Lacey 1996). Some other approaches are based on behavioural techniques, such as those involving teaching skills and breaking them into steps for learning. The emphasis given in this book is that this type of skills learning should retain the elements of choice and learner control identified in the interactive approaches. In the case study below, Dave successfully learned to find his way along routes from a teaching approach based on task analysis (small steps), but the accompanying relationship building and communication was in keeping with the notion of 'total acceptance of the person as an equal' (McGee *et al.* 1987).

Dave's case

When we first met, Dave spent most of his time at the back of his house picking moss out of the bricks. He had lived in a long-stay institution from age four and was then in his late twenties. Dave is blind, he has a hearing impairment and severe learning difficulties. It took a while for Dave and I to get to know each other, but we gradually learned that we shared a similar sense of humour and that we both 'knew our own mind'! This was a great discovery. I recognised from Dave's determined gestures and physical cues, e.g. squeezing my hand, a sort of impatience to get to do what he wanted. I started to follow Dave's lead and soon found that he was very quick at learning a range of skills if they involved things he liked e.g. he learned to turn on a tape player and adjust the volume to feel the vibrations, he learned to locate the mats and take his shoes off so that he could receive a foot massage, he learned to pour drinks. One of Dave's most liberating achievements was learning to walk upright and feel along a route. We experimented together, but it was Dave who showed me the best ways to teach him a route. The teaching approaches which I learned from Dave have often proved a useful starting point with other learners too.

Recording Recording learner involvement is vital. The individual learner may require considerable exposure to opportunities for 'having a say' before they are really able to do so. There is a danger that this may give the *appearance* of tokenism in the initial stages: 'although the fear of appearing to be tokenistic can be paralysing, some participation is better than no participation at all' (Simons 1999).

Effective planning and recording should clearly identify the process involved and provide evidence of progress towards fuller involvement and influence. It should be remembered that 'having a say' is a skill which requires practice. Enabling each learner to acquire this skill, in whatever form, is the responsibility of the learning provider (refer to sections on choice in Chapters 5 and 7 and assertiveness and self-advocacy in Chapter 4).

Learners will start at different levels of skill development in relation to choice and decision making, ranging from levels of awareness to levels of initiating choice (refer to Chapter 5). However, many learners with profound and complex learning difficulties may need to start at the point of developing awareness through close interactive work with a member of staff in order to establish a common ground based on 'respect, negotiation and participation' (Collis and Lacey 1996).

Recording learner responses, 'comments' and opinions by using video and photographs can provide a useful, accessible

Preethy's case

Preethy is in her late twenties. She has profound and complex learning difficulties and partial vision. She uses a wheelchair and is severely restricted in her range of movements. Preethy uses vocalisations, body movements and facial expressions to communicate, but when we first met, it seemed that everyone who knew Preethy was unsure about the meaning of her vocalisations and non-verbal communication. Her vocalisations and expressions often seemed to communicate distress, frustration and tension but sometimes the same set of circumstances elicited smiles and satisfied sounding grunts. Preethy and I spent time together 1:1 when she was out of her wheelchair. She seemed much more relaxed and comfortable on the floor. Over a period of time, we worked on contact through touch and 'talked' together using vocalisations. She often protested at being touched, so I respected her choice and tried again in a different way the next time. Progress seemed slow, but eventually we reached a point at which Preethy started to welcome interaction through touch. She started to reach out for me, make contact and laugh. Then, quite suddenly, she started to take the lead! She touched my hand, so I touched hers. She touched my arm, so I touched hers. The sequence continued until, finally, she pulled my face close to her and thoroughly explored my hair. These interactions were recorded on video and on paper (see Figure 2.4).

record of a learner's preferences and communication style. Sadly, people are sometimes sceptical of an individual's achievements. Many learners (myself included) behave very differently according to the situation and people involved. It is often difficult to convince sceptics if the learner is unable to reinforce claims of success by verbal accounts or standard tests. Photographic and video evidence can often win through, but all forms of recording and reporting are critical to ensure that the achievements of each learner are recognised and remembered.

Figures 2.4 and 2.5 show examples of extracts from recording sheets. A similar, but more detailed, recording sheet may be found in Hewett, D. and Nind, M. (1998) *Interaction in Action* (Figure 4.1).

Method	Responding	Initiating
Voice		ao sounds, varied pitch and volume
Face	smiled when I copied ao sounds	
Body		pushed his foot towards my hand
Eyes	stilled when I moved to his right line of vision.	

Figure 2.4   Example extract recording sheet

Choice Making

Today I chose: to go to the shop

From a choice of: shop or allotment

I made the choice by: taking the purse object of reference for shopping when offered the purse or the trowel

---

Figure 2.5   Example extract recording sheet

A responsive framework

It is important that indications of learners' views and preferences are recorded and fed into the ongoing review of the framework. While learners may be able to participate in review meetings and training in some ways, many learners with profound and complex learning difficulties may also require an approach that incorporates the chance to 'have a say' on a more day-to-day basis. So that these 'comments' are not lost, they should be recorded and used to inform a range of relevant processes, as exemplified in Figure 2.6.

Process	Example
Person centred planning	Records of Jill's choices showed that she participated more actively in groups of less than five people and that she worked most productively in 1:1 learning situations. She was subsequently offered a range of small group and 1:1 experiences and arrangements were made on the basis of her preferences.
Planning learning objectives	Learner evaluations showed that Michael enjoyed jazz music. During his college course, he learned to operate a tape recorder using a specially designed switch and he learned to use a colour sticker system to identify his favourite tapes.
Framework or curriculum planning	The records of evaluations from learners are reviewed alongside comments from carers, advocates and others, resulting in revisions to the framework, e.g. the prioritisation of 'relationship building' as a foundation skill (refer to Chapter 3) resulted from records of learner responses.
Organisation business planning	Positive responses from learners and increased requests from advocates and others indicated a demand for increasing courses run in community venues. This resulted in a change of focus in planning and funding allocations to facilitate a phased increase in community based courses over three years.

Figure 2.6   Examples of learners influencing planning

The framework for learning described in the chapters which follow is designed to facilitate a highly learner centred approach. The involvement of learners in the creative process of developing the framework is critical in ensuring that it grows and changes in response to learner needs and preferences. The focus of this chapter has been to illustrate the ways in which this can happen in practice, so that learners can influence, directly and indirectly, both hands on practice and curriculum and organisational planning. The framework for learning, described in Chapters 4–11, reflects its current state of development arising from learners 'comments' in recent years. It is an ongoing process.

Chapter 3

Foundation skills

This chapter outlines key aspects of development which are common to all the subject areas described in Chapters 4–11. It features brief comments and examples concerning those foundation skills which are not included in specific subject chapters. In addition, the 'core subjects web' (Figure 3.8), a map of links between the segments of each subject area and the foundation skills, has been included. It represents a way of thinking about joining all the elements of the framework together. It should be noted that foundation skills, like subject segments, are not mutually exclusive. In fact, some could be considered to be sub-sections of others. Figure 3.1 shows the foundation skills in diagrammatic form.

In order to ensure quality teaching/learning throughout the framework, all subjects also include: assessment of learning needs, abilities and motivation, appropriate functional positioning, comfort and security, adherence to identified strategies for supporting reduction of communication difficulties manifested in 'challenging' behaviour and use of a range of communication systems.

The foundation skills

Several foundation skills have been included in specific subject chapters to illustrate some ways in which they may be integrated under subject headings. These include:

Communication (Chapter 4)
Awareness of self and others (Chapter 5)
Exploration (Chapter 5)
Choice and decision making (Chapter 2, Chapter 5 and
 Chapter 7)
Purposeful movement (Chapter 9)
Cultural awareness (Chapter 10)

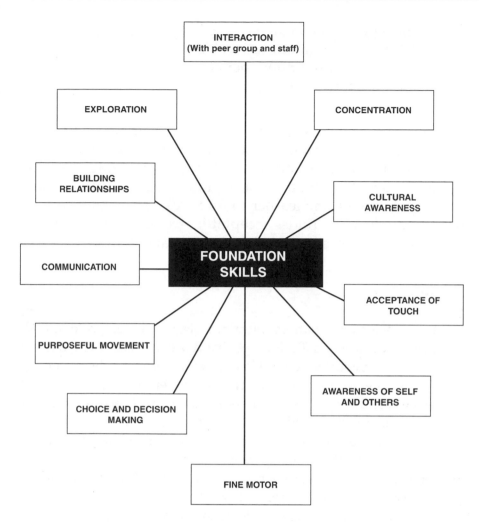

Figure 3.1 Foundation skills

Many learners with profound and complex learning difficulties require hand-over-hand guidance to learn, for which acceptance of touch is a prerequisite. Acceptance of touch can also open up new opportunities for the learner in relation to a range of development areas; such as, communication and relationship building, awareness and exploration. Touch can also raise self-esteem by making the learner (and staff) feel nurtured and accepted.

Some difficult decisions may need to be faced if the learner is expressing a choice not to be touched. Clearly, it is extremely important to respect learner choices. However, there are times when doing so would condemn the learner to continued isolation. The Further Education Unit (FEU 1992) suggests that we should think carefully about the following aspects when listening to choices:

Foundation skill: acceptance of touch (touch tolerance)

19

- 'time – perhaps you are not allowing enough time;
- the learners' communication skills;
- whether you are putting them or yourself at risk;
- your real motivation.'

(FEU 1992)

It should be remembered that the learner may have a life history of non-rewarding contact in which they may have experienced functional touch (e.g. bathing, changing) without positive interaction. Staff must explore touch sensitively and appropriately with the learner to find ways of making contact which the learner finds acceptable (refer to relationship building approaches opposite). This may take time.

David's case

David is a quiet man with an infectious giggle. He has profound and complex learning difficulties. He has a visual impairment, but makes use of residual vision in his left eye. He uses a wheelchair and enjoys being able to stretch out when out of it (he communicates this by smiles, contented sounds and relaxed body movements). Initially, David shrank away from contact and this made it difficult for him to participate in tasks. Assessments were carried out to find the best way to approach David. His responses were more positive if he was approached very slowly from the left and if sound or speech preceded gentle contact on his arm. During each visit to college, David spent some interaction time with me on the mats 1:1. Gradually, David learned that he could take control of the interactions, he started to initiate contact on my arms and shoulders and even traced his fingers on my foot in imitation of a foot massage.

Checklist for acceptance of touch:

- Ensure all contact is appropriate and respectful.
- Establish environment and tasks which motivate the individual.
- Allow time.
- Remain completely focused on the individual during contact time.
- Consider the best approach for each person e.g. approach from the side they see or hear best.
- Establish comfortable positioning which gives the learner maximum potential to move in order to initiate or respond to contact.

- Reflect on touch sensitivity, endeavouring to consider it from the learner's perspective.
- Talk about the learner's strengths and successes to enhance positive self-image.
- Monitor and record to facilitate analysis of the best approach and to evidence progress.

Figure 3.2 shows a recording format for acceptance of touch.

TYPE OF TOUCH	BODY PART	VERY RESISTANT	ACCEPT PASSIVELY	ENJOYS	SIGNALS FOR MORE	INITIATES
e.g. stroking	Right hand		[X]	[X]	[X]	[X]

Figure 3.2   Example of recording format for acceptance of touch (Bradley, 1991)

'Developing a relationship can be difficult and take a long time but it is a necessary basis for communication'

(Bradley and Snow 1994).

Foundation skill: building relationships

Building positive working relationships between staff and learners and between learners and their peers is complex with any group. The complexity is greater for many learners with profound learning difficulties. Communication difficulties, limited life experiences, physical and sensory difficulties and emotional issues may be some of the contributory factors.

This foundation skill holds as many challenges for staff as for learners because every relationship is unique and requires staff to work to a reflective or structured, yet highly creative and flexible, formula. In all areas of the framework, the first phase of contact between learners and staff should incorporate both assessment and relationship building prior to establishing learning programmes. Relationship building is allocated this priority position because without the subtle, interpersonal knowledge gained from it, it is difficult to ensure that learners with complex needs are engaged and consulted (see Figure 3.3).

Information

Refer to the video and handbook *Creativity with People with Learning Disabilities: Practical Ideas With and Without Equipment* (Allen and MacKay 1996) from Orchard Hill College (see References) for further examples of relationship building activities.

Aim	Practice Example
• communicate interest	Take time to say hello.
• communicate respect	Focus attention on learner, respond to his/her communication and choices. Record anything which might be an indication of choice e.g. eye flicker, frown.
• discover learner's interests and preferences	Record responses and focus on tasks the learner enjoys.
• spend time together	1:1 intensive work, directly supporting the learner in group tasks.
• be consistent	Always use a personal ID in all situations (e.g. watch, bracelet) to aid recognition. Establish a mutually comfortable structure for initial interactions e.g. greeting sequence (refer to Chapter 4). Endeavour to be consistently calm and responsive.
• ensure relationship building is rewarding for all involved	Learners are often accomplished readers of non-verbal signals: smiling, speaking in a pleasant tone of voice, projecting pleasure at being in the company of the learner.

Figure 3.3 Examples of staff roles in relationship building

Individual learning objectives in this area may include specific skills learning in addition to a more experiential approach. For example, a learner may decide to improve eye contact, learn to sign 'hello' or learn to initiate contact. The learner may also benefit from experiences which allow time for relationship building within a more fluid structure; such as, interactive massage, musical improvisation and intensive interaction. However, a structure of some sort, albeit a flexible one, is vital in order to ensure that both staff and learners can operate confidently within a clear context.

Some philosophies and approaches to learning which may be useful for relationship building are summarised in brief in the list below:

- Gentle teaching (McGee *et al.* 1987)
  Gentle teaching is based on humanistic philosophy. It emphasises the importance of bonding and developing relationships. It is a process which 'requires total acceptance of the person as an equal' (McGee *et al.* 1987).
- Interactive massage (Sanderson *et al.* 1991)
  '... communication and interaction can be developed through "Interactive Massage" where the primary focus of massage is to encourage responsiveness, interaction and

participation rather than aiming purely at sensory awareness ... relaxation or invigoration.' This approach uses touch as a means of developing trust and self-esteem. It aims to enable learners to progress through McInnes' and Treffry's (1982) eight stages of development:

1. resists
2. tolerates
3. cooperates passively
4. enjoys
5. responds cooperatively
6. leads
7. imitates
8. initiates

The aim of interactive massage is to achieve a more equal relationship between the carer/teacher and the learner. 'The support worker or carer initially gives much more and appears to receive little. As the relationship develops this is redressed as the individual becomes more responsive and involved in the relationship' (Sanderson *et al*. 1991).

- Communication through active music (Rodbroe and Hayes 1997).
  Based on music therapy and interactive techniques, this approach involves responding to the learner's sounds and movements using rhythms, sound and music. For example, Geoff vocalises, staff 'answer' with their voices or with a musical instrument. This approach can be extended to include use of lighting which is activated by sound.
- Responsive environment (Ware 1996)
  Based on child development research and everyday practice, this approach advocates making sense of learner's communicative behaviours through an understanding of the steps towards intentional communication:

  1. Voluntary behaviour (e.g. apparently random vocalisations)
  2. Purposeful behaviour (e.g. picking up a piece of equipment)
  3. Intentional communication (e.g. looks at you and smiles)

The approach incorporates reflective teaching. Staff are required to think about their interactions with learners, for example, their expectations, their observation and responses, sharing control with learners. There is also a need to consider the organisation of the session to make sure that staff attention covers each learner. The focus of the approach is to be very positive about learners and to have fun interacting.

- Intensive interaction (Nind and Hewett 1994)
  Based on mother–infant interactions, this 1:1 approach incorporates interactive playfulness in which the teacher may '[build] a game from an action, facial expression or sound made by the student' (Nind and Hewett 1994). The approach is highly learner centred. Staff are required to avoid 'dominating the classroom with our rules and choice of activity'. Instead, they take the lead from the learner by responding to any sound or movement the learner makes.

- Interactive approaches to teaching (Collis and Lacey 1996)
  This is a training programme for staff to explore interactive methods. It highlights the need for building relationships with learners in order to 'tune in' and learn about them. Staff are required to be effective at relationship building by achieving the following:

  - *Positively value learners and what they are doing (teachers are not superior beings).*
  - *Be receptive to the cues of students.*
  - *Be familiar with the interests, likes and dislikes of the learners.*
  - *Recognise interactive routines being established within the relationship which may form the basis of a rapport and eventually learning.*
  - *Develop shared understandings with students which will lead to new understandings.*

  (Collis and Lacey 1996)

One of the key aspects of relationship building, highlighted in all the approaches described above, is sharing control with the learner. It is important that learners are given a chance to lead, initiate and make choices within the relationship (see Sheila's case).

Recording

Close observation is required to monitor progress. Use of video recording can be invaluable in providing a prompt for reflection. It is difficult to record every aspect of this complex process, but progress in relation to identified specific skills and responses can be recorded. A diary of observations may also be useful. In particular, if the diary is written with reference to a

Sheila's case

Sheila is in her early twenties. She is vivacious. She has a strong love of music and is often tapping her foot, moving her body or making sounds to a beat. Sheila has profound learning difficulties and 'challenging' behaviours. Building a relationship with Sheila was a challenge, because she seemed to use her rhythms to shut out other people. I engaged in a series of relationship building tasks with Sheila and, gradually, she became more open to establishing a working relationship. One of the key moments was recorded on video. We were engaged in making hand rhythms, when Sheila made the discovery that she could lead the interaction. She took hold of my hand and moved it to control my hand rhythms. Sheila and I had established a relationship in which she felt supported rather than controlled. From this point, she began to focus on her non-verbal communication skills and the 'challenging' forms of communication gradually lessened.

checklist of things to look out for e.g. eye contact, responsiveness, acceptance of touch, initiating contact, recognition. One example of a recording format is given in Figure 3.4.

Recording for this foundation skill is likely to require a range of different formats to suit each learner. Some learners may have more advanced awareness and communication skills than others. For example, the focus may be on non-verbal indicators for one learner, recognition of personal objects of identification for another (e.g. Jane recognises Caroline because Caroline always wears three bangles), or verbal and signed interactions for another.

Foundation skill: interaction

Although interaction may be considered as a sub-section of communication and relationship building, it is given separate listing here since it is included as a segment in several subject wheels and is central to the group work which is a feature of many of the subject areas of the framework. The focus of this section is interaction between learners, rather than with staff. This is often difficult to achieve with learners with profound learning difficulties, since communication difficulties may be compounded by lack of immediate response to communication attempts.

Objective: to explore with Sheila non-challenging ways in which she can take control	
People involved	Sheila and Mike
Environment	multi-sensory room
Equipment	music only
Activity	movement
Date	23 June 2000
'Comments' from Sheila (what happened that might indicate what Sheila thought of the activity?)	Sheila smiled when the music started and when Mike started the patting game. She vocalised in indignant tones when he stopped patting. She appeared attentive but became lost in the music at times. She took over the lead in the patting game and then directed Mike to pat her back instead of her legs (by moving his hand).
Learning achievements	Sheila was able to sucessfully lead the interaction by vocalising and gestures. She did not need to use her 'challenging' ways of communicating, because the vocalising and gestures worked.
To do/not do next time	Continue. Try different music-varied rhythms. Try doing as part of group active music session. Encourage use of vocalisation and gesture interaction in other situations without music.

Figure 3.4 Example recording format

Examples of tasks for enabling interaction between learners

Pair work:

- Learners indicate who they would like to work with, e.g. by eye pointing, turning towards the person, naming, signing.
- Learners on mats: sometimes it is easier to interact more freely if not restricted by chair or wheelchair. A sequence of interactive tasks may be devised by experimenting and seeking response from the learners so that they have a say in defining the sequence e.g. touch hands, join hands, copy movements and sounds.

- Learners at a table or desk, e.g. cooking; doing art; tasks involving passing items to each other to complete.
- Learners at the computer.

Group work:

- Greetings rituals: Learners greet each other in turn, helped by staff if required e.g. touching hands, signing, naming.
- Hands-on-hands: Each person in turn places their hands on the pile of hands in the middle of the table. Then, the person with their hand on the bottom places it on the top, and so on.
- The wave: Pass rhythms, sounds, contact, movement round the circle by copying or 'replying'.

Note: The complexity of the task should be adapted to individual learning needs. Task examples given here are devised for learners with profound physical, communication and learning difficulties.

Chris, Julie, Wendy and Sue: a group case

This was a fun and lively group! Each learner in the group has profound learning difficulties, sensory impairment and 'challenging' behaviours. Positive interaction between learners was rare, but they had all made considerable progress in gaining appropriate communication skills and building strong relationships with staff. It was time to generalise those skills and facilitate some group bonding. One of the group activities used was 'hands-on-hands'. This involved the group sitting at a small table and piling each hand on top of others in turn. At first, the table was tipped, learners did not remain seated for long, hands were reluctant to touch. However, as the learners began to understand the structure of the task, they learned to anticipate their turn, they achieved greater spatial awareness and awareness of each other, they learned to coordinate their hand movements and locate by touch, and they became calm.

Recording

Recording may also be used as an opportunity for interaction by involving the learners in self and task evaluations (refer to Chapter 2). A group task, such as the hands-on-hands interaction in the case study, may involve recording of individual objectives and/or group objectives. See Figure 3.5 for an example of such recording.

Objective: each group member will lead part of the interaction			
Learner	Action	Help required	Next step
James	gave his hand to each person as greeting	staff guided his hand to reach out	reaching out hand without help

Figure 3.5   Example format for recording group objective

The role of staff in facilitating interactions between learners is fundamental to ensuring progression. 'It is not the learner who fails to learn but the teacher who fails to provide an adequate learning opportunity' (Collis and Lacey 1996). Staff working together in teams should be explicit about expectations that every member of the team will act to help learners to communicate, to progress, to choose and initiate learning and to participate in evaluating learning (refer to Chapter 2). Staff facilitating learner-to-learner interactions must be skilled in establishing the right conditions and then judging when to step

Barbara's and Tom's case

Both Barbara and Tom have been working 1:1 with staff over a period of time. Barbara has developed excellent eye contact and facial expressions, which she uses in a focused way for holding a 'conversation' with staff. Tom enjoys lots of physical contact. He initiates tight hugs and holding hands. Both learners have profound and complex learning difficulties. Barbara has severely limited movement. Both use wheelchairs. During a drama workshop, staff noticed that Barbara was attempting to gain Tom's attention with smiles and gaze. Staff responded by inviting them to 'sit' together. They were positioned closely on mats and cushions. In spite of careful positioning, Tom did not notice or respond to Barbara's attempts to interact. Eventually, staff asked Tom to pass some props (part of the drama) to Barbara. Staff helped Tom to do this by facilitating contact between their hands. Tom made eye contact with Barbara fleetingly. During the drama sessions which followed, staff continued to support the brief moments of engagement between them and interaction slowly increased. Barbara continued to initiate eye contact and, occasionally, Tom initiated contact by touching her hand.

back and allow the learners to take the lead or when further support is needed. Regular detailed evaluations of staff input are important so that details of practice are constantly reviewed and improved (refer to Chapter 1).

Fine motor (small hand movement) skills form an element of the basis of many of the development areas in the framework. Learners with physical restrictions may require adapted approaches and specific equipment to carry out fine motor tasks.

Foundation skill: fine motor

Examples of fine motor skills
grasp and release
pincer grip
posting

Examples of applications
holding a cup
picking up a button
putting video in slot

Julie's case

Julie is frail, gentle and friendly. She has profound and multiple learning difficulties. She communicates using excellent eye contact, smiles, head movements and movement in one arm. In order to gain greater control over her environment, Julie was introduced to a range of switch operated equipment. However, she did not have sufficient strength in her hand to operate many standard switches. A highly sensitive switch was used which responded to a light touch from her finger tips. Julie realised the connection between her movement and control of equipment (fan, light, computer) remarkably quickly. She smiled and her eyes twinkled in recognition of her achievement.

Some fine motor tasks lend themselves to a task analysis approach in which the task is broken into achievable steps which the learner practises, with appropriate support, until they are able to complete the task with the greatest possible degree of independence (Farrell *et al.* 1992). As with all aspects of learning, it is critical to ensure that the learner is given opportunities to indicate preferred tasks and approaches and that these choices are respected.

Example task analysis for a fine motor task

Reaching for and picking up a cup:

- learner picks cup up and takes to mouth with hands guided through;
- helper holds cup close to learner's mouth and guides learner's hand to cup;
- helper holds cup close to learner's mouth and verbally prompts learner to reach for cup;
- helper holds cup close to learner's mouth and waits for learner to reach for cup;
- helper holds cup further away from learner's mouth and prompts the learner as needed to reach for cup (this step may be repeated several times at distances further away from learner's mouth);
- learner picks cup up from raised surface on table (this step may not be necessary);
- learner picks cup up from table.

Refer to Chapter 11 for example of recording format for this type of objective.

Foundation skill: concentration

Some learners with profound and complex learning difficulties appear to focus on people and activities very fleetingly, with little apparent interest. In order to address this, it is necessary to review individual preferences and approaches to learning. As a foundation 'skill', this element of learning has been headed 'concentration'. In fact, the focus of development in this area in many respects relates more to motivation and awareness development, with increased concentration forming a benefit or outcome.

Checklist for helping learners to extend concentration

- Establish a quiet environment.
- Reduce distractions and interruptions.
- Provide 1:1 support for period of task.
- Give the learner your complete attention.
- Explain what is happening, use encouraging words and gestures e.g. 'Yes Claire, you're doing well.'
- Find tasks which the learner likes.
- Provide structure to tasks, but allow the learner to direct.

- Start at the learner's current level and build from there – short bursts of activity may be required.
- Use your interpersonal skills to keep the learner engaged i.e. smile, make eye contact, talk, make it apparent that you are fully involved and focused.

- Work at learner's pace.
- Record learner's progress and learner's evaluation of tasks (this may mean recording the learner's non-verbal responses) and adjust tasks accordingly.
- The learner requires regular and consistent opportunities to 'practise' concentrating.

Joseph's case

At first, Joseph seemed to shut off from the outside world and always positioned himself with shoulders hunched and head down. He has profound and complex learning difficulties and tunnel vision. He uses a wheelchair. Assessment showed that correct positioning of people and objects so that he could see them better was a key factor in gaining Joseph's attention. Once eye contact was established, he began to show awareness of his surroundings for brief moments. It was noted that he glanced more frequently at bright objects than others. Staff presented bright objects in varied ways and responded carefully to Joseph's every movement. Very gradually, he increased attention to preferred items and found the motivation to hold objects up to see them clearly.

Recording

It is often informative to record variables such as the activity and environment against the learner's attention and responses, in order to clarify the practice which best suits the individual. Figure 3.6 demonstrates this kind of recording.

The information in this section indicates the need to consider the best circumstances for learning for each individual. This will need to take into account the learner's current levels of awareness (refer to Chapter 5), motivation (preferred activities, conditions, people) and individual needs (e.g. hears best on left so need to position accordingly). It is attention to these elements of learning which provide the basis to enable the learner to increase concentration (see Figure 3.7).

Learner: Vicky	Date: 1 March		1:1: Sue
activity	computer garden game	watering with hose	planting in soil
time of day	11 a.m.	1.30 p.m.	2 p.m.
level of engagement	reached out to screen	turned head to sound of water	no apparent interest
concentration	45 secs	10 secs	[–]
comments	Check if lunch time medication could cause drowsiness. Try hose and planting tasks in morning to check.		

Figure 3.6   Example recording format

Date	Objective/activity/ people	Liked/disliked/ not sure	Showed preference by
3/5	1:1 interaction with JC	Liked	smiles, giggles, reaching out to JC
5/5	group music	disliked loud not sure soft	screwed up face, tension in body, turning away became calm when music was soft, body relaxed a bit Try soft only to see if likes.

Figure 3.7   Example motivation assessment extract

The core subjects web

The web diagram (Figure 3.8) shows a way of thinking about the elements of the framework joined together. The close links between development areas identified in each part of the framework and in the foundation skills facilitate smooth transition between courses for learners enrolled in more than one subject area and allow individual learning objectives to be reinforced across a range of learning opportunities and in different settings.

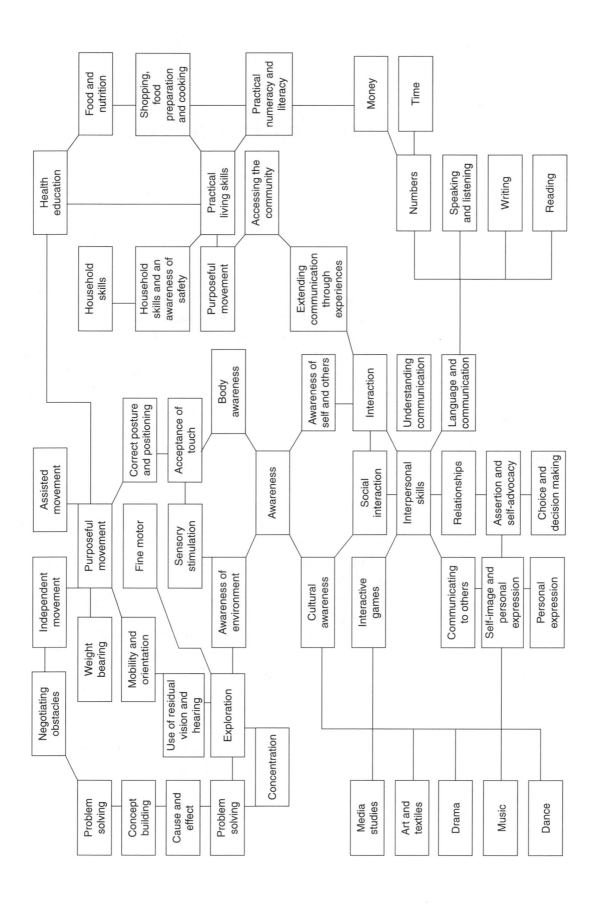

Figure 3.8 The core subjects web

Chapter 4

Communication development

This subject area aims to promote all aspects of interaction and communication, both non-verbal and verbal.

As in all areas of the framework, it is essential from the start to focus on establishing relationships and finding out about the learner's likes and dislikes (refer to the foundation skills in Chapter 3).

Introduction The focus of this chapter is to examine the process of communication and to consider how effective communication takes place. The chapter will look at methods of conveying messages, at the barriers that prevent messages from being received or understood and at ways of breaking down these barriers to enable 'shared control of an interaction where both people involved in the communication act are influencing the outcome' (Bradshaw 1998).

The segments of the communication development subject wheel referred to here are: 'communicating to others', 'understanding communication' and 'assertiveness and self-advocacy' (Figure 4.1). The remaining segments of the wheel are considered elsewhere in the book.

In addition to the main subject area, additional studies may be offered in:

- *Interpersonal skills*: To provide a variety of social opportunities in which individuals can interact verbally and non-verbally
- *Personal expression and assertiveness*: To facilitate increased confidence in initiating communication and individual self-expression.

Figure 4.1 Subject wheel

'Communication is the exchange of information by any means possible' (Bradley 1991). It is about conveying a message of some kind. It is a two-way process in which there is a giver and a receiver of information. For communication to be successful, the message that is sent needs to be clearly understood and this requires specific skills by both parties.

Although speech is the most obvious form of communication it is important to recognise, particularly in the context of adults with profound and complex learning difficulties, that information can be effectively conveyed and clearly understood without it.

A definition of communication

Information

For ways of assessing communication methods, refer to the training package by Helen Bradley (1991) *Assessing Communication Together* (see References).

Methods of communication

Everyone has the ability to communicate. A good starting point for ensuring successful communication is to consider the ways in which we all communicate messages to one another. For simplicity these can be broken down into the use of voice, facial expression, eye contact and body language.

Julia's case

Julia is a wheelchair user with limited body movement and no speech. To learn more about Julia's methods of communication staff recorded her use of voice, facial expression, eye contact and body language. Here is a summary of our observations:

Voice
Julia makes a soft 'aaaagh' sound in response to a lively and humorous atmosphere. She makes a contented 'gurgling' sound when sitting with the group and strong positive vocalisations accompanied by broad smiles when familiar members of staff sit next to her for a chat. 'Oooh' sounds suggest an enjoyment of an activity and loud vocalisations appear to indicate excitement during 'live' music.

Facial expression
Julia smiles in response to various group activities. Sometimes the smiles are particularly broad, most noticeably during group music. Julia grimaces in response to unexpected loud noises.

Eye contact
Julia returns eye contact when spoken to and initiates contact with others by turning her head to look at them.

Body language
An animated movement of one leg and her head suggests excitement or that she is really focused on an activity. This has been particularly evident during body movement exercises.

The benefits of recording methods of communication

Spending just a few minutes on a regular basis recording someone's methods of communication is a good way to learn more about how that person is able to respond to and initiate communication. In Julia's case staff learned more about the people she enjoyed being with and her preferred activities. This informed planning for future provision. Julia went on to access music therapy and joined a creative studies course where she had further opportunities to develop her communication skills through music and movement.

There is a further significant benefit to recording methods of communication in the way described. By focusing on specific aspects of communication one is more inclined to provide further opportunities for communication to take place and there is a greater possibility that any sound or other signal made by the learner will be acknowledged and acted upon.

Teaching tip

To maintain a flow of communication when recording detailed observations consider using a video camera or having a second person as an observer to fill in the recording sheet. Involve the learner in recording too (refer to Chapter 2).

Learning through experiential interaction

Many learners, like Julia, have limited obvious forms of communication and may appear difficult to 'reach'. For these learners, experiential interaction approaches maybe the first stage to 'find a way in'.

Intensive interaction (Nind and Hewett 1994) provides opportunities for interactions to take place and develops communication skills in difficult to reach learners by giving meaning and value to any attempt at communication. Learners are given opportunities not merely to respond but to lead interactions with their own chosen method of communication (refer to Chapter 3).

Signs and symbols

There is a range of more formal sign and symbol languages and communication systems that can be taught. Some examples are:

- Objects of Reference – objects used to represent an activity, place or person (for example: a cup = drink, a small paintbrush = art). Refer to Figure 4.5.
- Makaton and Signalong – language programmes using signs derived from British Sign Language.
- The Standard Manual Alphabet – a two handed manual alphabet used for finger spelling.
- The Deaf Blind Manual Alphabet – similar to the Standard

Manual Alphabet but with letters spelt out on the learners' hands.

(For further information on signing systems, see References and Useful Addresses at the back of this book.)

Spoken language	Sign	Object of reference
1. 'Hello'	Makaton 'Hello'	
2. 'It's John'	Makaton sign 'my name' and then Finger spell 'J'	Show personal identity e.g. wedding ring
3. 'Would you like a drink?'	Point to learner Makaton 'drink'	Show a cup

Figure 4.2   Greeting sequence

Choosing the right approach

The choice of teaching approach is dependent on the learners' needs and preferences. Often it is beneficial to reinforce communication by using a range of methods in a structured sequence. For example, the greeting sequence in Figure 4.2 includes speech, signing and objects together:

A checklist for responding to and encouraging communication
- Allow time and space for communication to take place.
- Create an environment within which communication is consistently taking place between all people.
- Respond and give meaning to sounds and movements. Try echoing or imitating.
- Interpret communication signals and tell the person what you think they are saying.
- Consider whether one sound or movement indicates a whole message. The same sound could also mean different things in different contexts.
- Establish a dialogue of sounds, words, signs or movements, within which you are equal partners.
- Use any methods of communication that work.
- Create opportunities for others to lead the conversation.
- If a person has vision, encourage them to look at your face and encourage eye contact.
- Use knowledge of an individual but don't have a predetermined idea of the outcome of an interaction.

- Keep a record of observations and share information with other people in an individual's life.
- Do not assume a person cannot understand if they are unable to express understanding.
- Do not assume that habitual communication is meaningless.
- Look at your own methods of communication. Could you simplify your own message if necessary?
- Consider whether your communication is meaningful to the learner.

Barriers to communication

For some people there may be considerable barriers to overcome before they can be in a position to attempt to communicate. It is helpful to consider what these barriers might be for both the 'giver' and the 'receiver', when developing strategies for communication.

There may be physical barriers such as general discomfort, limited movement or a sensory impairment. Personal barriers too may exist, ranging from shyness, fear, dislike or a personality clash. An individual's readiness to communicate may also be affected by general distractions and interruptions and by his or her physical and mental well-being as well as their past experience of communicative situations.

Organisational structures can create barriers too, for example, time constraints and limitations on opportunities for interaction.

Overcoming the barriers

Creating the circumstances for effective communication to take place requires flexibility and a consideration of the individual's:

- barriers to communication;
- understanding of language;
- ability to use different methods of communication;
- particular interests and likes.

Example:
Before Jack embarks on a learning programme with a new group of people staff consider the notes in Figure 4.3. Based on these, Jack needs:

- to participate in activities in the morning;
- to be in a responsive and vocal group, ideally with Steven;
- to participate in 'live' music, perhaps music therapy.

barriers	understanding	methods used	interests/likes
Not able to move his arms and legs. Visually impaired. (See assessment.) Gets tired in the afternoon.	Responds to his name. Shows an understanding of some familiar words and phrases (see communication profile).	Moves head and vocalises in response to sounds e.g. laughs, cries. Echoes words and says 'Yes'/'no' in context (but not consistently).	Social contact. Music. Finds 'loud' groups stimulating and responds well to a vocal peer group. Friends with Steven (a student in the college).

Figure 4.3   Communication in relation to Jack as an individual learner

The broad learning objectives are:

1. To develop Jack's ability to respond to and initiate communication through vocalisation, head movement and facial expression.
2. To provide further opportunities to develop his vocabulary.
3. To provide opportunities for Jack to make informed choices.
4. To investigate Jack's ability to use a head switch in order to switch a cassette machine on and off.

The importance of communication within the framework

The ability to communicate is critical to all aspects of learning, particularly for people with profound and complex learning difficulties. Communication underpins the entire framework and is both a core subject and a foundation skill. In practice, this means keeping a strong focus on communication through individual learning objectives, session aims, routine practice etc. For example, objects of reference in every teaching area help learners to make choices and to anticipate events.

Communication cannot be taught in isolation and skills learned and developed on the course are reinforced and extended in other core subject areas.

A range of communication approaches is used in all aspects of the learners' life in order to establish and build quality relationships and there are many examples of this throughout the book. Although difficult to quantify, compared with skills-based programmes, Hewett and Nind (1998) note that 'staff who become competent at promoting incidental interactions with a person are also more likely to become competent at achieving scheduled sessions with that person where necessary.' In David's case, earlier interaction work has enabled him to participate in a more structured, objective-led learning programme.

David's case

David is autistic. He is a self-contained man and rarely looks directly at people or objects. He attended a communication development course during which a 1:1 interaction programme was devised to improve his ability to make eye contact. By the end of the course David had made considerable progress in terms of the frequency with which he was observed to give fleeting eye contact during interactions.

In addition to extending his interactions with others, David has been able to use this skill in other areas. On a science and technology course he has begun to independently operate the computer by looking at and touching the touch screen to create patterns. This is enabling him to learn more about cause and effect and has given him a new interest.

David's case demonstrates the benefits of interactive approaches in providing a route for establishing the skills, experience and confidence which may lead to developments in other areas.

In developing structured skills-based task analysis programmes. such as pouring a drink or learning a route, the ability to observe and adapt methods used according to the learners' responses to the programme is essential (refer to Chapter 11).

Assertiveness and self-advocacy

'The essence of self-advocacy is being able to exert some control and influence over your life, and at a basic level this will involve indicating needs and desires, rejecting and refusing things, and making choices that matter' (Sanderson 1995).

Enabling adults with profound and complex learning difficulties to acquire further assertiveness and self-advocacy skills requires learning programmes to develop communication skills and providing situations that will enable them to use these skills to take control. In the previous example, Jack developed the skills that would enable him to decide when to turn music on and off by operating a head controlled switch. Jack was also able to make more choices as staff became better at interpreting his communication methods.

Susan's case

Susan has profound learning difficulties. It was difficult to determine her understanding or use of communication because she cut herself off from others by vocalising loudly and covering her ears. She loves water. A bowl of water was introduced. Susan would splash her hands in the water and over several weeks a member of staff would do the same, talking gently to her and, taking the lead from Susan, introducing brief periods of close contact. Susan began to accept and later initiate eye contact and hand to hand contact. Her more relaxed facial expressions and positive vocalisations communicated the message that she was enjoying this shared activity and was becoming increasingly relaxed in the company of the member of staff. This was the first step towards building her communication and self-advocacy skills. Subsequently, Susan has begun to use objects of references to anticipate events and make choices.

Susan has since successfully completed an Integrated Studies course (refer to Chapter 6) working alongside pupils at a local mainstream school, where she showed an increasing interest in those around her by giving eye contact for up to a minute at a time. She was consistently prepared to greet others by reaching out to touch hands and showed her increased interest through eye contact and positive facial expression during interactive activities and music. In the last few weeks of the course Susan actually began to sing!

Susan went on to receive an 'Outstanding Achievement Award' to publicly acknowledge her work at a special ceremony held at the College.

Recording progress

Recording should provide evidence of progress towards the development of communication skills and indicate successful approaches which may be used by others. To ensure accuracy, recording should be done at the time or immediately after communication takes place. The recording sheet will need to be simply laid out so as not to impede the process of communication, while allowing for specific details to be noted so that progress can be accurately monitored.

Figure 4.4 shows an example of Susan's recording sheet for a five minute interaction.

Date	Eye contact				Hand contact			
	Fleeting		Sustained (2 secs +)		Fleeting		Sustained (2 secs +)	
	accepts	initiates	accepts	initiates	accepts	initiates	accepts	initiates
3/3	/////	/	/		/			
9/3	////	//	///	/	//	/	/	
10/3	/////	////	//	/	//			

Facial expression		Voice		Body		Comments
tense	relaxed	negative	positive	tense	relaxed	
///	/	////		/////		Fairly consistent acceptance of fleeting eye contact. Increasingly relaxed. Starting to accept more close contact and has begun initiating contact. Is less comfortable with hand contact at present.
///	//	//		//	/	
//	//	/	/	///	///	
//	///	/	///	//	////	

Figure 4.4 Recording sheet for communication

It is critical for staff to develop their own communication skills in order to support the development of these skills in others. Involving the whole team through regular staff training develops good practice and produces a shared sense of ownership. Here are a few suggestions:

Staff training ideas

1. *Brainstorm methods of and barriers to communication in staff meetings.*
2. *Role play situations around communication without speech.*

Introduce objects of reference

As a staff team, decide on a number of core objects of reference to use throughout your place of work. The choice of objects will be determined by the needs of the group and will be influenced by the weekly timetable of activities. Objects of reference may be chosen for activities (e.g. cooking and shopping) and places (e.g. the bathroom), see Figure 4.5.

Decide what the objects of reference will look like. Each object of reference should be small, accessible, easy to acquire and duplicate, and safe to explore.

Teaching tip
Store core objects of reference together in all the main teaching or living areas. Ensure each object is clearly identified.

> **Information**
>
> For further guidance about objects of reference, refer to Keith Park's article (1998) in RNIB's Focus newsletter or Adam Ockleford's (1994) book on objects of reference (see References).

Objects of reference should be used consistently by all practitioners working with the individual, i.e. the same objects should be used at home, at College, at the club, at work etc.

Activity/Place	Object of Reference
Gardening	Trowel
Kitchen/Cooking	Wooden spoon
Bathroom	Flannel
Art	Small paintbrush

Figure 4.5   Examples of objects of reference

Introduce signing

As a whole team compile a list of ten to twenty core signs for your place of work. These will be signs that you intend to use regularly (in addition to signs for specific individuals) and should be chosen in accordance with the needs of your learners. Some example are 'Hello/Good', 'Yes', 'No', 'Drink', 'Toilet', 'What', 'Where' and 'Which'.

Regularly practise signing in staff meetings by revisiting the core signs and later by introducing more signs. A good way of doing this is to practise signs around a theme, for example, food or animals. If you are feeling particularly brave, try sitting in a circular formation and create a story with each member of staff taking turns to move the story on with a sign.

This Chapter outlined some of the key components of the Communication Development subject area. As a foundation skill, communication is featured throughout the framework. Each of the subject chapters which follow includes elements of communication development. The interconnection across the framework is represented diagramatically in the core subjects web at the end of Chapter 3.

Chapter 5

Science and technology

This subject area aims to develop awareness, exploration skills and informed decision making, thus maximising the learner's control over their environment.

As in all areas of the framework, it is essential from the start to focus on establishing relationships and finding out about the learner's likes and dislikes (refer to the foundation skills in Chapter 3).

'Awareness is the foundation for learning . . . Awareness is not, however, understanding: It is the point from which understanding can begin. Bringing about more understanding and therefore more control, is part of the learning process' (FEU 1992).

Introduction

This chapter considers the learning process in relation to all segments of the science and technology subject wheel (Figure 5.1). It investigates methods of observing and assessing learners and suggests activities, strategies and recording methods to facilitate progress and understanding. The final section provides an overview of the foundation skill choice and decision making. Other aspects of choice and decision making are explored in Chapter 7.

The focus of the chapter is to show how the segments of the subject wheel link to each other. Segment definitions build upon each other and often the same activities can be used to provide a range of opportunities for learners to develop skills at levels appropriate to their individual needs.

In addition to the main subject area, courses are also provided in:

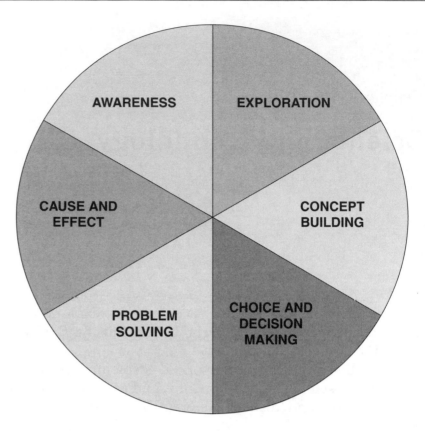

Figure 5.1   Subject wheel

- *Information technology*: To use computers and other technology as a means of enabling learners to maximise their control over the environment.
- *Environmental studies*: To provide learners with sensory experiences relating to the natural environment and to develop those skills required to participate in gardening activities.
- *Design and construction*: i) To provide learners with the opportunity to select the project of their choice and to develop the understanding that individual steps will lead to an end product. ii) To develop skills required to work in wood and other materials through the correct use of appropriate equipment.
- *Food and nutrition*: To develop awareness of food: its origin, preparation and nutritional value, through a range of practical and sensory experiences.

A definition of science and technology

The Collins Dictionary (McLeod 1995) defines science as 'the systematic study of the nature and behaviour of the material and physical universe'. Merriam-Webster's Online Dictionary (2000) defines science as 'the state of knowing: knowledge as distinguished from ignorance or misunderstanding' and technology as 'the practical application of knowledge especially in a particular area.'

For learners with profound and complex learning difficulties, study and knowledge of 'the universe' will relate to situations, objects and events within their experience. They will need support, guidance and structured learning experiences in order to interpret and understand situations. This will involve building relationships and clarifying communication in order that they can share control of these interactions (refer to Chapter 4). Those who help to facilitate this knowledge and its practical application need to provide stimulating and challenging environments and use strategies which enable the learner to explore and experiment with confidence.

Structuring activities and experiences

Gardening activity: sand and water

Equipment:

- large bowls of dry sand, wet sand, cool water, warm water, soapy water;
- jugs, sieves, water sprays, sponges, spades, spoons, flannels;
- towels, talcum powder (removes wet sand without irritation).

Learners are introduced to the sensory properties of the sand and water on hands and feet – touching, stroking with sponges or flannels, with hand-guided help, by pouring, sprinkling or spraying. They are encouraged to place their hands or feet into the bowls, or to investigate and explore independently.

Staff monitor and record the learners' responses and actions.

We need to assess in order to establish whether an individual can benefit from what can be made available. It is necessary to design an assessment which meets our learners' needs at the point and place where they are, both geographically and cognitively. It should be remembered that relationship building and assessment should be developed together (refer to Chapter 3).

Assessment

Marvin (1998) states that, 'It is important that staff increase their sensitivity to their pupils' behaviour and work towards becoming masters of observation.' She suggests that they observe changes in areas such as movement, expression and appearance.

Information relating to learner's responses may be recorded as in Figure 5.2.

Activity	Level of awareness – how demonstrated
Dry and wet sand poured and sprinkled over hands.	No response – remained calm and passive.
Warm and cool water poured and sprinkled over hands.	No response – remained calm and passive.
Dry sand poured and sprinkled over feet.	Mandy gasped and widened her eyes – not apparently distressed. Activity repeated several times – same reaction – eventually laughed too.
~~Wet sand poured and sprinkled~~ over feet.	~~Mandy pulled her foot away and made~~ an apparently distressed sound – facial expression unhappy – returned to dry sand activity.
Comments/next time Appears to show preference for touch on feet and more awareness. Dry sand preferred – Try other textures on feet.	

Figure 5.2   Example recording format for assessing responses

Assessment is a tool for identifying learner preferences, choices and learning requirements. It should provide a baseline from which learning priorities and objectives can be established.

An initial assessment may be made using the format shown in Figure 5.3.

Baseline assessment	Consider – movement, expression, appearance, verbalisation
What activities did _____ participate in today?	How did _____ make this choice of activities?
What did _____ like today?	How did _____ show this?
What didn't _____ like today?	How did _____ show this?
How did I share this with _____?	Next time we'll do . . .

Figure 5.3   Baseline assessment

In order to ensure that assessment and recording give us accurate information about learners and provide us with a baseline from which to develop and extend their learning we need to consider the following:

- The learner should be physically comfortable: correctly seated and supported where necessary; wearing comfortable clothing; warm or cool enough; situated in sufficient, comfortable and functional lighting.

  'It is hard to learn if you are falling out of your chair . . . It is hard to learn if you are hot, have the sun shining in your eyes and are wearing shoes two sizes too small for you'

  (FEU 1992).

- The learner should be comfortable with the person they are working with.
- There should be no distractions.
- Environmental conditions may affect the learner's responses – context, time of day, where they are working, who they are working with.
- Activities should be repeated a few times on different occasions to check responses and to check our interpretation of those responses, ask others.
- Warn the learner that something is going to happen. Communicate what is taking place, use language, touch, sound, movement, objects of reference etc.
- The learner may need short bursts of involvement. '"Continuous provision of learning opportunities" does not mean that the longer you teach, the more your students learn' (Campbell *et al.* 1996).
- Allow the learner to set the pace. Give sufficient time for him/her to explore and investigate.
- Let the learner lead the learning experience.
- Use recording to assess what is of relevance and interest to the learner and develop learning opportunities accordingly.

Facilitating learning

For learners to achieve awareness they will need to develop intentional responses to sensory stimulation. 'Information received through the senses can be considered as the basis for an individual's learning about and acquiring a conceptual understanding of the properties of the physical world' (Warren 1994).

Awareness

Mandy's case

Mandy is a gentle, quiet woman who shows limited positive responses to sensory contact from others. She is thought to have no hearing as she does not show any response to sound. She has visual impairment, responding only to extreme changes in lighting or to a bright light being shone directly near her. She is very resistant to touch, particularly on her hands and near her mouth, pulling or turning away if she is approached too quickly. Jim works with Mandy, taking things very slowly, sitting close beside her and speaking to her so that she can feel his breath on her face. He lightly touches her hands or feet before introducing new sensations to her and repeats his actions a few times so that she becomes familiar with the routine. Mandy remains relaxed and accepts dry and wet sand, warm and cool water being poured and sprinkled over her hands. She shows no response. When Jim pours dry sand over Mandy's feet she gasps and her eyes widen. She does not appear distressed so he continues. Mandy's reaction is the same. After a few times she smiles and laughs. Jim tries with the wet sand – Mandy makes an unhappy sound and pulls her foot away. Jim returns to the dry sand and Mandy relaxes and smiles again for the duration of the activity. Jim finishes by rubbing Mandy's feet with a towel and drying with talcum powder.

Mandy is demonstrating awareness and a possible preference for touch on her feet. Jim will need to continue to assess Mandy's responses to a range of experiences in order to extend and develop her understanding.

Exploration Learners with profound and complex learning difficulties will need structured opportunities and support to encourage them to investigate all aspects and properties of objects and situations in order to maximise their understanding of their experiences.

Byers (1998) suggests, 'It is possible to use a sensory approach to facilitate the development of functional learning strategies, such as observation, anticipation, prediction and the use of memory.'

Dev's case

Dev is involved in sand and water activities, working with Carla. He can be quiet and withdrawn, choosing to spend brief moments of involvement in activities interspersed with short walks around the room. Carla encourages Dev to feel the water and sand being poured over his hands. He walks away and returns a number of times, holding out his hand to receive the substances. He watches intently as they are poured, then watches them run off his skin. Carla continues with her work each time Dev has a short walk, talking about what she is doing all the time. She pours water and sand through a sieve. Dev returns to watch closely. Eventually Dev comes to sit at the table. He puts his hands into the bowls, investigating the properties himself. He takes a variety of containers, filling and pouring independently. He gets up for a walk and returns to continue with his exploration. Carla talks to Dev about what he is doing and what is happening.

Dev is exploring the properties of sand and water. Carla will need to respond to Dev's responses, actions and interactions and thus extend his experiences in future sessions, allowing him to take the lead in his investigations. She may need to ensure that he is able to explore outside or in an area where he can use sand or water more freely without causing any safety hazards such as wet or slippery floors and surfaces.

Dev's exploration skills may be recorded as shown in Figure 5.4.

Activity	Level of involvement 1 = low, 5 = high	Time of exploration	Type of exploration
Sand and water poured over hands.	4	45 secs – 1 min each time – returned several times.	Observed Carla – watched water and sand intently as they were poured – looked at hands as sand or water rolled off.
Sand and water poured through sieve.	4	As above	As above
Independent exploration	5	Up to 3 mins at a time – returned several times.	Independent exploration – hands in sand and water pouring, sieving.
Comments/next time: Continue with sand and water exploration – extend to feet – possibly work outside – buckets, spades, brushes, hoses, sprays.			

Figure 5.4 Example recording format for exploration

Cause and effect

Byers (1998) advocates that learning opportunities should 'encourage purposeful exploratory and investigative behaviour by creating significant and stimulating links between actions and effects.'

> ### Martin's case
>
> Martin is a sociable young man who enjoys the company of others. He is able to grasp and release small objects but has limited arm movement. Each week his session starts with an interactive group game. Sometimes the game is Boccia, which involves releasing a ball down an adapted tube which staff or learners can hold and direct at skittles or a tower of tin cans. Martin particularly enjoys the game when it is played with tin cans. He takes his turn and releases the ball down the tube, stills his body, waiting for the crash as the cans fall and then laughs with pleasure. As the game progresses and Martin takes another turn, he pushes the ball down the tube and immediately smiles and covers his ears in anticipation of the clattering sound. Again he laughs as the tins crash to the floor.
>
> Martin's actions are demonstrating his understanding of cause and effect in a manner that is clearly enjoyable and rewarding for him.

Concept building

A concept is an understanding of the properties of an object or a situation gained though experience.

In order to make sense of the world we live in we need to be able to experience, to investigate and to build concepts. Adults with profound and complex learning difficulties will often need continuing support to gain these experiences. They will require structured activities which will enable them to explore, understand cause and effect, solve problems and thus build concepts. Concept building is essential in order to make informed choices and decisions or to exercise control over the environment. To offer a choice between jam or Marmite means nothing without understanding of the 'jam-ness' of jam and the 'Marmite-ness' of Marmite.

Indira's case

Indira is a lively, energetic and sociable woman with a visual impairment. She likes to spend time out of her wheelchair in a matted area independently investigating a range of equipment with interesting textures. Over time staff have observed that she shows a preference for objects which have some degree of floppiness and which make a sound as she flicks them, in particular fabric covered bean bags and a large rubber textured disc. Indira has extended her investigation of these objects from feeling with her hands, holding between her teeth as she flicks them, to throwing them on to the floor, after which she stills and listens to the sounds they make.

Indira is exploring, developing her understanding of cause and effect and thus building her own concepts of these objects and their properties. She is also making choices about the objects she wants to work with.

Problem solving may be understood as the ability to arrive at a solution to a problem through observation, exploration, experimentation, hypothesis and testing.

Problem solving

Alan's case

Alan enjoys craft activities involving quite intricate skills: cutting complex shapes, making collages, colouring intricate patterns, threading. He has autistic spectrum disorder and likes to work at his own pace in a quiet area. The group were making Christmas decorations (stars) for the tree. Alan's job was to make holes in the decorations using a hole punch and then thread ribbon through. Alan watched as Karl showed him how to punch a hole in one corner of the star then took the equipment to a table to work alone. Karl watched his progress. Initially Alan tried to push the star too far into the hole punch. The points were not under the punchers and he was unsuccessful. He tried again – no luck. After a few tries a hole appeared at the edge of one of the points, but it was still not right. Alan turned the hole punch upside down and pressed it repeatedly to watch how the mechanism worked. He then fed one point of the star into the punch and under the metal puncher so that a hole appeared in the right place. Alan was then able to punch all the other stars accurately using this method.

> Alan used observation, exploration, awareness of cause and effect and his concepts of the objects he was working with. He made a hypothesis and tested it in order to solve the problem to his satisfaction. Karl provided an environment in which Alan was able to see the task through at his own pace and in his own way. Karl observed Alan's actions giving verbal encouragement where appropriate and was ready to offer help and guidance if required.

Suggestions for activities

One activity can provide opportunities for learners to develop skills at levels appropriate to their individual needs. Figure 5.5 gives examples:

Activity	Skills
Cookery	*Awareness* – offering smells, touch, tastes, experiencing vibrations of mixer. *Exploration* – smelling, feeling, tasting, sieving, stirring, pouring. *Cause and effect* – cracking an egg, making toast, watching the changes in appearance of food as it is mixed or cooked. *Problem solving* – opening tins and packets, weighing and measuring, dividing mixture equally e.g. between cake cases. *Concept building* – through the above. *Choice and decision making* – which tasks to take responsibility for, what to cook, how to present the food.
Ball activities	*Awareness* – textured balls rubbed over skin, sounds of balls bouncing or being hit, 'jingle balls', PLANET flashing balls (see Useful addresses). *Exploration* – sizes, textures, sounds, rolling, throwing, bouncing. *Cause and effect* – throwing, bouncing, catching, hitting. *Problem solving* – directional throwing, aiming, hitting, catching. *Concept building* – through the above. *Choice and decision making* – size and type of ball, type of ball activity, which role to take e.g. bowler or batsman.
Gardening	*Awareness* – offering equipment, soil, water, seeds etc. to feel, smelling herbs, flowers, vegetables, observing, tasting, holding the garden hose. *Exploration* – feeling, smelling, pouring, using spades, rakes, brooms, watering cans. *Cause and effect* – watering cans, digging, sweeping, picking flowers, lawn mowers. *Problem solving* – picking ripe fruit and vegetable planting, weeding. *Concept building* – through the above. *Choice and decision making* – choice of what to plant, which container, which activity, how to carry it out, who to work with.

Figure 5.5   Example activities

The ability to make and demonstrate informed choices and decisions.

The FEU document *Developing Self Advocacy Skills with People with Disabilities and Learning Difficulties* (1990) states that the core components of self-advocacy include:

- being able to express thoughts and feelings with assertiveness if necessary;
- being able to make choices and decisions;
- being able to make changes.

When talking about effective self-advocacy, Griffiths (1994) states that important factors include the provision of:

- an understanding of choice;
- a better understanding of the world, its possibilities and difficulties;
- the development of skills and competencies;
- a feeling of confidence;
- a feeling of being encouraged and supported as they develop towards autonomy.

Choice and decision making begins with awareness that one object or situation is different from another. The 'chooser' needs to have a concept of the options available, an understanding that a choice is being offered and a mutual system of communication which will ensure that their choice is respected and acted upon.

The continuum detailed in Figure 5.6 shows progression from skills of awareness to those of choice and decision making and provides a framework for assessment and objective setting.

Choice and decision making

AWARENESS
- Has structured experiences of people, objects or events.
- Passively participates in structured experiences or events.
- Demonstrates awareness of people, objects or events.

RESPONSE
- Responds consistently to various stimuli.
- Responds in different ways to people, objects or events.
- Responds consistenty to identified people, objects or events.
- Initiates interactions with people, objects or events.

EXPERIENCE OF CHOICE
- Has structured experiences of a range of choice.
- Demonstrates likes and dislikes and indicates a preference.

AWARENESS OF CHOICE
- Makes a choice between or indicates a preference for people, objects or events immediately experienced.
- Demonstrates awareness of cause and effect.

ASSISTED CHOICE – between two objects, people or events
- Demonstrates a choice between two objects, with guidance.
- Illustrates a choice through a shared form of communication.
- Makes an occasional choice, with guidance.
- Makes limited choices more consistently, when prompted.
- Makes a choice independently when two options are presented.

INDEPENDENT CHOICE
- Makes an independent choice, when offered, from a limited range of options.
- Makes an independent choice when options are offered.
- Makes an independent choice when asked to make a choice or decision – option free.
- Initiates and/or indicates independent choices and/or preferences.

Figure 5.6   Development steps from awareness to choice

Chapter 6

Community studies

This subject area provides opportunities to develop the skills and experience required for participation in community life.

As in all areas of the framework, it is essential from the start to focus on establishing relationships and finding out about the learner's likes and dislikes (refer to the foundation skills in Chapter 3).

Adults with profound and complex learning difficulties are living increasingly within the community. The process of building skills and confidence in the 'real world' is vital when enabling adults to develop a way of living that is empowering. This process is not always easy. 'We are only just learning how to work with people as equals and partners: how best to enable people to develop new skills in the places they are needed – at home, at work, in the community; and how best to support people to develop a lifestyle of their own, unencumbered by our own and society's prejudices and fears' (Wertheimer 1996b).

This chapter examines some of the practical issues for building social skills, life skills and vocational skills in the community. It focuses on a number of aspects: building skills and confidence in 'real' environments; developing interaction in community settings; using themes, e.g. shopping, to develop skills and experience, and developing vocational skills through community-based work experience. See Figure 6.1 for the subject wheel.

In addition to the main subject area, an 'additional studies' course is also provided in Integrated Studies, which is designed to provide opportunities for students to develop positive relationships through combined work in a variety of settings.

Introduction

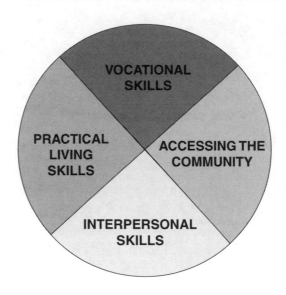

Figure 6.1 Subject wheel

Building skills and confidence in 'real' environments

Teaching skills in a structured environment, such as a college or other setting, allows the teacher or helper to create predictable routines that enable learners to take control and make choices. Learning within the community is more difficult to structure and, as a result, provides challenges to both the learner and the teacher or helper.

Sometimes learners require learning to take place within the college or a similar environment in the first instance, so that they can access close support to build skills, confidence and understanding. During this time, teachers and learners can establish a relationship and identify the type of support the learner needs. Learning is then transferred to 'real' environments when the learner is ready and confident. This step-by-step approach can be used to bridge successfully the gap between specialist provision and inclusive opportunities. Learners, particularly those with communication difficulties, physical needs and 'challenging' behaviour, may require transitional or long-term support from specialist teachers, or others with relevant expertise.

It is important to remember that 'confidence-building is . . . crucial to the development of independence' (Sutcliffe 1990). To establish this self-confidence, particularly within the community, it is necessary to reject purely skills-based models. One of the prerequisites for learners with profound and complex learning difficulties is to find out the way in which individuals communicate, and to build relationships that enable mutual understanding of learners' preferences.

Communication may be subtle and idiosyncratic, for example slight body movements, or facial expressions (refer to Chapter 4). The building of experience in a variety of community situations and environments is an essential element in this process.

If learning is to take place, elements of structure are also essential. An example of this structure could be to establish regular 'signposts' during the course of a community trip as shown in Figure 6.2.

The need for predictable routines and signposting is determined by individuals' needs following an initial period of assessment. As learners develop experience, confidence and skills within the community, reliance on these signposts may be reduced. Moving from a structured to a less structured environment can also be made easier by focusing in the structured environment on routines and skills that are likely to be used in the community, for example turn-taking, recognising food and drinks, self-advocacy, and choice-making.

The importance of selecting activities and environments that are motivating to the individual cannot be overstated. It is essential that learners play as large a role as possible in the decision making process. Initially this may require a process of trial and error, with individuals trying out a range of activities in a number of community environments. Accurate recording of achievements and responses in various environments allows learners' choices to be recognised and built upon. This also enables learners and staff to build trust and confidence together in new environments.

Activity	Possible signposts
1. Greeting	Use of Makaton, photos, group games.
2. Travelling	Object of reference, same music in car, regular bus stop, sit next to familiar person, consistently point out familiar landmarks.
3. At venue	Regular route, having favourite foods and drinks, familiar activities.
4. Returning	Sit in chosen seat, goodbye signs and routines, evaluation by learners.

Figure 6.2 Examples of 'signposts'

Checklist for choosing community venues and activities:

- *Access*: Is the venue or activity accessible to students with a variety of needs? Can the activity be adapted?
- *Motivation*: Are there opportunities to participate in activities that are motivating for the individual? Does the venue/activity provide interesting and achievable challenges? Can students choose venues/activities themselves? e.g. through experiencing a range of activities and assessing responses.
- *Safety*: Has a risk assessment been carried out before visiting a new venue or beginning a new activity? Remember, 'taking some measured risks is important in supporting people to achieve a wider range of life's goals' (McIntosh 1999).
- *Inclusion*: Are students able to participate in 'real-world' activities? What are the opportunities for building links with individuals and organisations in the community? What are the needs in terms of information, training and support for individuals or groups in the community? What support is needed by community organisations in order to work with learners?
- *Age appropriateness*: Is the venue/activity 'appropriate to the person's age but . . . meaningful to them'? (McConkey 1998).

Developing interaction in community settings

Community settings provide a wide range of opportunities for individuals to develop awareness and interaction with others. McConkey (1998) finds that 'various researchers have reported heightened animation and communication in people with profound disabilities who experience increased participation in community activities.'

Enabling learners to develop awareness, and facilitating interaction, requires a sensitive approach from those supporting them in the community. This approach involves three main elements:

- building trust and communication;
- effectively advocating individuals' hopes and wishes;
- enabling individuals to participate as independently as possible.

McConkey (1994) suggests that one of the most common problems reported by members of the public in their dealings with people who have a 'mental handicap' is 'not knowing what to say to them or how to react'. For those supporting learners in the community this means that part of their role must be to effectively and respectfully interpret individuals' communication to others in the community. However, teachers and helpers must be careful not to communicate *for* learners. Structuring opportunities so that learners can communicate successfully is important.

Gary, Catherine and Sandra: a group case

All three learners have profound learning difficulties, and have been part of a group who join a drama class at the local mainstream FE college. In different ways, all three learners lack confidence in community settings. Prior to joining the drama class the group practised a range of group games in the structured environment of the specialist college, and visited local cafes where they were able to choose and purchase refreshments. The mainstream college was visited on a number of occasions prior to joining classes in order to use the canteen and allow the learners to become familiar with the environment. Joint planning ensured that group activities practised in the specialist environment were included in the drama class at mainstream college. As learners have become more confident, staff support has become more discreet. Gary now regularly locates the working area and canteen independently at college; Catherine leads musical activities; Sandra hands money to the cashier in the canteen independently.

Checklist for developing interaction in the community

- A prerequisite is to develop knowledge of learners' communication, and build relationships based on mutual understanding.
- Focus on developing simple 'user-friendly' communication. Make sure as many people understand these communication methods as possible.
- Concentrate on 'core messages' which cover common interactions.
- Allow learners to take the lead. Sometimes confidence is built when those supporting individuals 'step back'.
- Respect the learner as they are. Do not apologise for, or be embarrassed by, unusual communication.

- Provide opportunities to practise skills e.g. repeating activities, preparing in less pressured environments.
- Focus on one or two activities at a time, with progression achieved either through extending this range of activities, or building skills in one area.
- Create opportunities for learners to build relationships with individuals e.g. re-visit shops, pubs, leisure facilities to enable recognition and trust-building.

Information

Refer to the curriculum support materials by Equals (tel. 0191 2728600) and by ALL (tel. 02476 470033 Ext. 4263) for ideas about skills that can be developed in a range of community settings (see References and Useful addresses).

Using themes to develop community involvement

The process of building the learner's experience in a range of community environments and situations is dependent on the context within which an individual is living. Community experience is very different in rural and urban areas for example. Themes can be used by those supporting individuals in order to ensure them access to a wide range of community activities. Many activities will cross themes. They may be used as a starting point for exploring aspects of community life.

Examples of themes are:

- shopping
- community services
- sport and leisure
- the arts
- travel and transport
- the environment
- food and drink

Focusing on one of these themes, shopping for example, will highlight how each learner can build confidence and involvement. Shopping can provide opportunities to develop a wide range of skills. The table in Figure 6.3 shows examples of ways in which learning objectives can be achieved through 'shopping opportunities'.

Learning objectives must reflect individuals' needs and abilities, and should be simple to understand for both learners and staff. Finding items to purchase that the learner values is also important.

Refer to Chapter 10 for further information about developing themes.

Sunil's case

Sunil is a young man who enjoys being outdoors, especially when the weather is good. He enjoys food and drink. He is visually impaired and has profound and multiple learning difficulties. Sunil has participated in regular weekly shopping trips, and over time has developed a wide range of shopping skills. He is able to locate and pick up a shopping basket independently and on his own initiative when entering the supermarket. He can take items from the shelves to put in the basket with light physical assistance only, hand coins to the cashier at the checkout and pack a carrier bag with verbal and gestural reminders only. Sunil has developed his shopping skills very gradually. Further skill areas were introduced to him when a reasonable level of confidence and competence was achieved in areas already practised. In order to increase motivation and involvement, shopping trips were linked to Sunil's favourite activities by finishing with a drink in the supermarket cafe or a picnic in summer.

Learning objectives	Shopping opportunities
Developing choice and decision making.	Using photos to identify and pick items, making shopping lists, choosing shopping venue.
Developing understanding and use of language.	Verbally highlighting a small range of items to be purchased, pointing out selected environmental features.
Developing eye-contact and hand–eye coordination.	Locating, picking up shopping basket and food items.
Developing sequencing skills.	Set procedure at checkout e.g. carrying basket to checkout, unpacking and paying for items, carrying bag to bus.
Gaining experiences of smell, touch, taste.	Touching cold food items, smells at the bakery, fish counter, feeling food packaging.

Figure 6.3   Achieving learning objectives through shopping

Developing vocational skills

For many adults with learning disabilities, the last 15 years has witnessed a growth in work opportunities. Supported employment schemes, such as MENCAP's Pathway Employment Scheme have enabled many adults with learning disabilities to participate in a variety of real jobs in integrated settings. However, according to Wertheimer (1996a), few agencies have been 'supporting people with severe or profound learning disabilities, additional physical disabilities or communication difficulties.' Work must be seen as a realistic option for adults with profound learning difficulties, if appropriate to the individual. As with the building of community skills and experience, colleges and other settings can provide a crucial link to enable learners to develop vocational skills and work experience.

The building of vocational skills must focus on the assessment of the learner's strengths, motivation and needs in relation to work-based activities. This assessment must be, as Wertheimer (1996a) suggests, 'very different from the "functional assessment" approach', requiring 'a combination of sensitive observation, creative thinking and inspired guesswork'. Through establishing work-based activities within the college or other setting, learners then have the opportunity to practise skills and discover motivating activities. Careful recording of learners' participation in a range of work based activities is vital in order to establish learner preferences and to evidence progression. Griffiths (1994) advocates enabling learners to 'sample a range of vocational areas before actually committing themselves to employment'. The development of vocational skills is educational in itself and can widen the horizons of learners and those supporting them.

Skills can be developed through a range of work-based activities, as seen in Figure 6.4.

Example of Work-based Activity	Potential Skill Development
1. Cafe – learners set up and run cafe.	Kitchen skills (laying tables, tidying up, washing up), presentation and social skills, shopping skills, recognition and use of money, choice-making (e.g. what to sell), awareness of food and personal hygiene.
2. Clerical Work – learners carry out a range of office-based tasks.	Fine motor skills, concentration, ability to follow instructions, IT skills.
3. Gardening – learners carry out variety of gardening tasks.	Physical skills, team/group work skills (e.g. passing items, asking for help).

Figure 6.4 Examples of skills which can be developed through work-based activities

Having discovered each learner's potential and preferences during these work-based activities, the next step is to set up opportunities for community-based work experience.

Susie's case

Susie is a sociable and humorous woman who has lived in institutional care for most of her life. She has profound learning difficulties and uses a wheelchair. She is able to use one arm, and can carry out a range of activities such as holding a cup and cutlery independently, and skilfully operating her electric wheelchair. She communicates using a small number of single words, but understands much more. After attending a year-long part-time college based vocational skills course, Susie began a work experience placement at a local library, supported 1:1 by a college tutor. She worked for 45 minutes each week, carrying out a range of tasks such as stamping dates into books and stacking books onto low shelves. After carrying out this placement for a term, Susie then moved to a local charity shop where she has been for almost a year. Her job there includes sorting items and arranging them for display and taking money and placing it in the till. She has developed good relationships with other workers, all of whom know her name. After work experience each week, Susie likes to visit a local cafe to have refreshments.

Checklist for establishing work experience placements

- Provide opportunities for the learner to visit the workplace prior to beginning work experience.
- Consider carefully the level of support needed in the workplace. The prime aim should be to enable the learner to carry out tasks at work and experience opportunities for interaction.
- Ensure that those supporting the learner know him/her well, and are confident in a community environment.
- Establish exactly what is expected when at work; tasks to be carried out, health and safety issues, clothing to be worn etc.
- Find out who is responsible for insurance when at work.
- Be sure your expectations are realistic in terms of time spent in workplace and tasks carried out. A measure of success is whether the learner wants to return next time.
- Provide opportunities for the learner to develop

relationships with other workers. The checklist outlined earlier in this chapter for developing interaction in the community is equally relevant in a work context.

Teaching tip
The learner can keep a record of his/her work experience through a photographic collection. Include details of the journey to work, who the learner works with and the range of tasks carried out. This record can be used as a part of the learner's c.v.

Conclusion

Building skills and experience in the workplace is likely to be a slow process for people with profound and complex learning difficulties. The need for support from a job coach/college tutor means that opportunities for extending time spent in the workplace may be limited. While adults with profound learning difficulties may be unlikely to work full-time in paid employment at the present time, the value of work for many should not be underestimated. Griffiths (1994) comments that work provides 'a way of shedding one's disabled status and joining the normal world of workers'. Many people with profound learning difficulties will continue to require access to education and other provision in order to gain further skills and experiences in addition to their work. This multiple options model provides the potential to meet the needs of learners by providing the structure and support as well as the opportunities required to participate in community life. The model demands a high level of collaboration between service providers, employers and others (refer to Chapter 12). Building links with local supported employment organisations is one example of the importance of collaboration in enabling adults with profound learning difficulties to enter the world of work.

Chapter 7

Life skills

This subject area aims to develop practical living skills which will enable each individual to participate with a greater degree of independence in everyday life.

As in all areas of the framework, it is essential from the start to focus on establishing relationships and finding out about the learner's likes and dislikes (refer to the foundation skills in Chapter 3).

The chapter will look at four segments of the life skills curriculum wheel (Figure 7.1):

- Food and nutrition
- Health education
- Household skills/Awareness of safety
- Shopping, food preparation and cooking.

The other Life Skills segments are discussed in Chapters 4, 6 and 8 of the book. Within the food and nutrition section of this chapter, opportunities for choice and decision making will be explored. Issues relating to accreditation for learners with profound and complex learning difficulties, within the context of a life skills framework, are explained in brief at the end of this chapter.

Introduction

Food and nutrition

Aim: To develop an awareness of food; its origin, preparation and nutritional value, through a range of practical and sensory experiences.

Food and cookery can be an excellent means of providing sensory experiences. A cookery activity for adults with

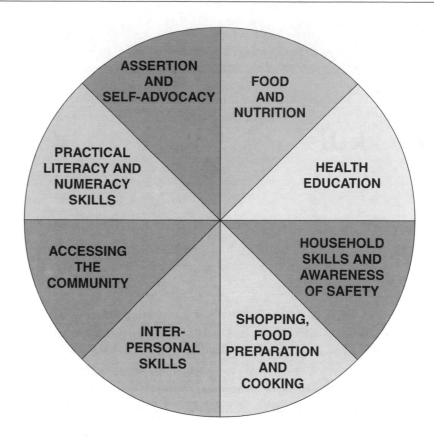

Figure 7.1   Subject wheel

profound learning difficulties can be planned to be age appropriate, relevant and motivating. It can often be a good starting point for gaining information about a learner's strengths, needs and preferences.

Sensory perception is an integral part of everyday activity. People with profound learning difficulties, in particular those with sensory deficits, may be unable to acquire a satisfactory level of stimulation from their surroundings. Additionally, they may be confused and overwhelmed by the impressions they receive, and may be unable to make sense of the incoming information. It is crucial therefore that we think carefully about how we structure and present information to learners with profound learning difficulties.

Some key points for planning food-related activities

- Don't attempt too much: the total involvement of a learner in making a banana milkshake is more valuable than rushing him/her through a complicated lemon meringue pie recipe.

- Think about your aims: if you want a cookery activity to be a vehicle for sensory exploration, then the entire process of making a Christmas pudding might be appropriate. If, however, you want to teach a learner to cook something independently, then cooking a shop-bought Christmas pudding in a microwave would be more appropriate.
- Recipes with short cooking times can be useful to allow the learner to be involved in the complete sequence: preparing and cooking food, watching/smelling it cook and sampling the end result fairly soon.
- Photograph ingredients and end products, to facilitate future choice making.
- Involve the learners in choosing recipes for subsequent sessions.
- Make the task of following a recipe more accessible to learners by putting together photographic/symbolic recipes.
- Put together a themed recipe file e.g. fruit recipes/fish recipes so that learners may become familiar with food types.

Dinah's case

Dinah enjoys noisy, lively activities. She sometimes loses interest when working on quiet activities which go on too long. Dinah has profound and complex learning difficulties and a visual impairment. She finds food very motivating, but long recipes have proved to be unsuccessful. The cookery slot was reduced from 30 minutes to 10 minutes and some very simple recipes were introduced which required only one or two ingredients, or one step to prepare. e.g. toast, milk shake, orange juice (squeezed fresh oranges), yoghurt and raisins, crackers and cheese.

Dinah coped well with a short, focused cookery slot and remained motivated to practise the following:

- raising her head for longer periods;
- opening her hand to hold/explore objects and ingredients.

Making choices

Choice making is the right of every individual but it requires acceptance by each member of the multidisciplinary team that choices made by a person with PMLD are as valid as the choices we ourselves would make in similar circumstances.

(Tilstone and Barry 1998)

The life skills subject area offers numerous opportunities for learners to make choices. For many learners with profound and complex learning difficulties, food can often be a good starting point because it is:

- concrete: you can see it, touch it, taste it, smell it;
- relevant: most of us eat every day, it is within our daily experience;
- immediate: the outcome of making a food choice (i.e. the chosen food) can usually be experienced straight away;
- motivating (in most cases).

There are many ways in which choice can be incorporated into structured food-related learning experiences. This is most successful in a learning environment in which choice 'events' are carefully planned and recorded (see Figure 7.2).

To enable learners with profound learning difficulties to make choices:

- identify current opportunities for making choices;
- consider preferences;
- negotiate long-term and short-term choice objectives with the individual learner;
- plan method of recording choice 'events';
- plan for choice making within session structure/plan;
- plan less, achieve more;
- allow adequate time;

Activity	Opportunities for choice
Shopping lists	• Use real food, packages, photographs to choose what to buy. • Choose purse/wallet/bag. • Choose member of staff to shop with.
Shopping	• Use photographs to choose where to shop. • Choose items by looking at/pointing to/picking up/vocalising. • Choose flavours e.g. ice creams.
Preparation and cooking	• Choose who does what (use objects of reference: wooden spoon = cooking; sink brush = washing up). • Choose which food to prepare e.g. fruit salad or drinks? • Choose a fruit to explore/prepare for the fruit salad.
The meal	• Where to sit/who to sit next to/eat alone or with a group. • Choice of food. • Choice of drink. • Yes or no to background music.

Figure 7.2 Food-related choice events sequence

- make it relevant and meaningful;
- do not offer a choice unless it can be followed through;
- evaluate short-term objectives;
- negotiate further objectives to balance consolidation of skills with progress.

Refer to Chapter 5 for further information on choice.

David's case

The planning element of meal preparation enables learners to choose, buy and cook lunch ingredients. David is motivated by practical tasks. He has severe learning difficulties and profound hearing loss. The process of choosing at 9.30 a.m. what to have for lunch at 12.30 p.m. was confusing for David, and frequently resulted in him becoming distressed, and communicating in a challenging way. Staff were keen that David should have the opportunity to choose his lunch, but were asking him to make a choice out of context. By offering David his choice at lunch time, the correct context and relevant clues enabled him to succeed. Staff could easily plan for this choice by having an additional main dish, vegetable or sweet available, to enable David to make his choice.

John's case

John is working towards becoming more involved in making small, day-to-day choices. He has profound and complex learning difficulties and limited vision. His planned choice opportunity is to choose cheese for crackers. John samples a small piece of Edam and some soft garlic cheese. When both are offered a second time, John closes his mouth tightly to the Edam but opens his mouth for the garlic cheese.

Aim: To develop an awareness of issues relating to health and well-being.

Health Education is concerned with quality of life and with the promotion of the physical, social and mental well-being of the individual. It involves not only imparting knowledge about what is beneficial and what is harmful but it also

Health education

involves the development of skills which will help individuals to use their knowledge effectively.

(Eales 1991)

Health education covers much more than personal care and sex education; it is concerned with enhancing and developing the learner's self-esteem, in order to enable him or her to be more involved in their own health and well-being. Within a flexible curriculum framework, Health education may be promoted as a single course, in addition to being 'integrated' into other subject areas. The delivery of any health education programme requires a flexible approach, which takes into account the sensitive and confidential nature of issues raised.

Graham's case

Graham enjoys practical activities. He has profound learning difficulties, and often appears quite nervous. A measuring activity was used to enable Graham to practise the negotiated learning objectives of:

- increasing awareness of others in the group/remembering names;
- developing self-esteem and confidence in order to try new activities.

The learners and staff measured each other, and plotted comparative heights on the wall. Photographs were taken for follow-up discussion. Graham began to anticipate the task of measuring others in the group by pointing to people, and picking up the pen.

The Towards Independence module 'Knowing About Myself' was used to accredit the course work (ASDAN, Award Scheme Development and Accreditation Network, see Useful addresses).

An example health education programme for adult learners with profound and complex/severe learning difficulties consists of:

- body awareness;
- awareness of self and others;
- exercise (see 'Information' below);
- healthy eating (see case study example below);

- dressing/undressing;
- personal care;
- sexuality issues.

Information

For adapted yoga exercises and training, refer to:
'You and me Yoga' (Gunstone 1993) Tel: 01524 782103
'Yogacise' (ASDAN Towards Independence module)
Tel: 011 7946 6228.

The aim of the healthy eating topic is for learners to be aware that different foods provide various nutrients within the diet, and that it is important to eat a balanced diet for good health and well-being. 'If people are to move to more independent lives they will need to practise planning their own diet, and making healthy choices for themselves.' (Rodgers 1998)

Suggested content of a healthy eating topic:

- fruit and vegetables;
- meat and fish;
- pasta, rice, potatoes, cereal and bread;
- dairy food;
- 'naughty' food! e.g. cream cakes.

Learning opportunities in a healthy eating session: Fruit topic

- exploring the sensory elements of fruit: looking, feeling, smelling, tasting;
- identifying fruit;
- choosing fruit to taste;
- passing fruit around the group: interacting with others;
- matching/sorting/categorising fruit e.g. putting all the apples together/distinguishing between fruit and dairy products;
- exploring photographs of fruit/matching to real fruit;
- putting together photographic or symbolic shopping lists;
- shopping for fruit: in a greengrocers/supermarket;
- cooking with fruit.

Group case: George, Lucy, Andrew

Individual learners in the group are working towards achieving negotiated learning objectives:

- George is developing hand–eye coordination skills, he is focusing on looking at and feeling the fruit.
- Lucy is beginning to use photographs to make choices, she is focusing on matching fruit to photographs.
- Andrew is developing his interpersonal skills, he is focusing on passing and receiving fruit to/from others in the group.

Information

Literature about food and nutrition/healthy living can be obtained from:

- health awareness leaflets (from GP's surgery/clinic/chemist);
- specialist books e.g. *Nutrition By Design* (Hurst *et al.* 1995);
- health specialists e.g. nurse, dietician.

Household skills and awareness of safety

Aim: To develop a range of household skills which can be used in a variety of settings and to develop an awareness of health and safety issues.

Household skills can be an easily accessible component of the life skills subject area. It does not require specialist equipment and can be experienced almost anywhere, on a day-to-day basis. The content of the household skills segment is quite broad and includes tasks which are likely to be practised on a regular basis e.g. wiping tables, and tasks which may be experienced less frequently e.g. using the washing machine. Within the household skills segment, there are opportunities for liaison between home and services, in order to ensure that skills are practised consistently in appropriate contexts (refer to Chapter 12).

Learning to be aware of health and safety issues is an important part of enabling more independent living, and should be included in all appropriate subject areas. Some examples are included below.

Some examples of kitchen guidelines	Associated topic ideas for learners with profound and complex learning difficulties
• Wash hands before you touch/ prepare food.	• awareness of hands • clean/dirty
• Use oven gloves when putting things in/taking out of oven and microwave.	• awareness of hands (include exploring different types of gloves) • hot/cold
• Do not touch any electrical equipment with wet hands.	• wet/dry • explore a range of switch-operated equipment • cause and effect
• Take care not to scald yourself with hot water (kettle, hot water tap).	• hot/cold • wet/dry

Figure 7.3   Examples of kitchen guidelines

Group case: Sid, Monique and Ricky

Household skills/Awareness of safety. An activity example:
Three learners are developing individual skills while participating in a single group activity. The activity is based on 'hot and cold' with a long-term objective of 'increasing awareness of health and safety issues'. Hot and cold items, e.g. hot water bottle, frozen peas, ice cream, tea, are passed around the group allowing adequate time for touch and taste. This needs to be done safely and yet conveying to learners the dangers involved.

- Sid is choosing which items to pass around the group.
- Monique is increasing her experience of exploring objects.
- Ricky is exploring a range of items to highlight his preferences.

Information

'Moving On' (Equals 1999b) describes a continuum of nine levels of participation within a home management course, for learners with profound learning difficulties (see References).

Shopping, food preparation and cooking

Aim: To develop skills associated with meal planning, shopping for food, cooking, serving and enjoying a relaxed social meal.

The life skills subject area provides a context within which many learning opportunities can take place. This particular segment enables learners to participate in a sequence of life skills activities, and provides an opportunity to see a task through from beginning to end.

The sequence of activities begins with a planning element; planning what to eat, what ingredients to buy, where to shop, how much money to take, how much time to allow. Planning is quite an abstract process, and this can be difficult for learners with profound and complex learning difficulties. 'Time', in particular, is a difficult concept to understand. The planning process can be made more concrete by using objects of reference and other communication cues as appropriate e.g. when planning what to drink (and buy) at lunch time, the use of drinks bottles, 'hot drink' containers, as well as photographs, makes the 'planning' task more concrete and accessible.

Learners may be encouraged to develop and use literacy and numeracy skills through activities such as preparing shopping lists, counting money, estimating how much money is needed, telling time, counting items of food and cutlery. Food is also an excellent medium for introducing learners to the notion of sharing the experiences of each other's cultures. It may form part of a theme or range of other experiences related to different cultures (refer to Chapter 10).

Shopping

Shopping provides learners with the opportunity to access community facilities, and to use and apply acquired literacy and numeracy skills in a practical way. It provides broad social contact, the opportunity to convert preferences and choices made at college into reality, and is a means of extending learning experiences beyond the 'classroom'. Learners are enabled to participate in every aspect of shopping through various means of communication, including spoken and written, signing, symbols, pictures, photographs, and objects of reference.

Money-related activities do not focus solely on numeracy skills, but provide opportunities to develop much broader skills which may be helpful for learners with profound and complex learning difficulties (see case study below).

Refer to Chapter 6 for further information on shopping.

Group case

In a life skills course, shopping/money activities are being used to provide opportunities for learners to practise specific skills:

- Colin's long-term objective is to develop counting skills. A step towards achieving this objective is to count out five one-pound coins.
- Dan's long-term objective is to become more tolerant of 'waiting' situations. A step towards achieving this objective is to wait for change at the checkout.
- Helen's long-term objective is to increase opportunities for making choices. A step towards achieving this is to choose a purse to take shopping.
- Alan's long-term objective is to increase confidence with new people. A step towards achieving this objective is to hand money to the cashier.
- Jenny's long-term objective is to develop interpersonal skills. A step towards achieving this is to collect purses from others in the group.

Accreditation

The Further Education Funding Council Inspectorate Report (1998–99), states that Awards are most effective when they 'enable students to gain confidence and self-esteem by giving recognition for their achievements' (FEFC 1999).

An effective curriculum for adults with profound and complex learning difficulties develops from the needs of the learners, into appropriate and relevant curriculum or teaching areas. In addition to providing an external validation of learner achievement, accreditation should also support and enhance the existing curriculum. If accreditation is allowed to lead the curriculum, then learners may follow a rigid, pre-set programme of work which will not be based on individual need. This may result in the accreditation of activities which are of little significance to some learners.

There are several routes of accreditation available for learners with learning disabilities and difficulties. For example Award Scheme Development and Accreditation Network (ASDAN) Workright; ASDAN Towards Independence; The National Open College Network; ALL; Equals. Appropriate accredited routes for learners with profound and complex learning difficulties are fewer. Some of the above may be appropriate, but need to be selected carefully or adapted. 'Awards which enable students to learn through practical activities rather than through theory are the most effective' (FEFC 1999).

A record of experiences, participation and progress, for those learners not working on accredited courses, provides a valuable internal validation of achievement. Additionally, 'recognition can be achieved on a day-to-day basis, through the development of a positive organisational culture, which makes commonplace celebration of every achievement, large or small' (Allen 2000).

Orchard Hill College outstanding achievements awards ceremony

Some examples of non-accredited learner achievements are:

- increased confidence in interacting with others;
- successfully finding own way around an unfamiliar environment (learner with visual impairment);
- increased willingness to participate in tactile activities;
- consistently activating an adapted switch to operate a tape recorder;
- increased willingness to make eye contact with other learners in the group;
- increased participation in group activities.

The Awards Ceremony is an annual event. Learner achievements are recognised and celebrated through the presentation of certificates and sharing with family, carers and others.

Checklist for ensuring accreditation is suitable

- Choose the most appropriate accreditation route and modules.
- Select modules which will enrich and enhance existing courses.
- Adapt modules/activities according to the needs of the learner. If a module needs a lot of adaptation, it may not be appropriate.
- Select accreditation routes and modules which recognise and celebrate the smallest achievements.
- Do not attempt too many modules.

- Allow adequate time to complete a module, and work at the pace of the learner.
- Repeat and reinforce learning experiences, if relevant.
- Use the accreditation regional meetings as an opportunity to meet regularly with other professionals/share good practice.
- Look carefully at the abstract/physical requirements of a module: some may not be appropriate for learners with profound and complex learning difficulties.
- Negotiate long-term and short-term objectives with the learner and establish the most appropriate route for meeting them, either with or without accreditation.

Chapter 8

Basic study skills

In this subject area we aim to develop skills in maths and English, from learning to match a shape, to writing and number skills.

As in all areas of the framework, it is essential from the start to focus on establishing relationships and finding out about the learner's likes and dislikes (refer to the foundation skills in Chapter 3).

Introduction This chapter takes into consideration a wide ability range. Examples of teaching activities that are relevant to learners with profound and complex learning difficulties are featured.

The six segments of the subject wheel in Figure 8.1, together with the foundation skills described in Chapter 3, form the framework for the subject area. In this chapter we will consider five out of the six segments: interpersonal communication, reading, writing, time, and number. Money has been included in life skills in the previous chapter.

The National Curriculum stresses the benefits of studying English and mathematics. 'The study of English', it says, 'enables (learners) to express themselves creatively and imaginatively and to communicate with others effectively.' It describes maths as equipping us 'with a powerful set of tools to understand and change the world.'

The skills to be learned must be realistic and above all relevant to learners with profound and complex learning difficulties. Tasks must be focused, with clear objectives appropriate and motivating for the individual. Much of the initial task may be working towards literacy and numeracy skills, familiarising the learner with new experiences and

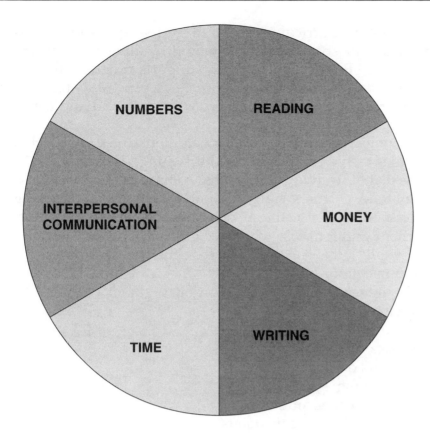

Figure 8.1   Subject wheel

patterns of working and making aspects of the wider curriculum accessible to the learner.

Checklist for choosing tasks and materials for learners with profound and complex learning difficulties

- Assessment: which skills will the learner develop?
- Motivation: will the learner find the task interesting?
- Relevance: how will these skills benefit the learner's life?
- Presentation: is it clear what the learner is expected to do?
- Monitoring and evaluating progress: how will this be observed and recorded?
- Adult status: does the task respect the learner as an individual adult learner?
- Equipment: does the learner require specific or adapted equipment in order to access the task?

The sections which follow introduce some practical approaches to suit learners with a range of learning difficulties, including those with profound and complex learning difficulties.

Interpersonal communication

The National Curriculum states that, 'Teaching should ensure that work in speaking and listening, reading and writing is integrated.' Progress in one area supports progress in another and is often dependent on it. This is especially true when considering the needs of learners with profound and complex learning difficulties.

Many learners rely on non-vocal alternatives to speech and visual or tactile clues to aid with listening. Aherne *et al.* (1990) stress that, 'Effective interpersonal communication includes the use of tone, gestures, signs and body language ... Learning to understand and use these social aspects is important for all (learners) and for those who have little or no use of speech they are vital' (See Chapter 4 for further information on communication skills).

The interpersonal communication segment consists of the following elements:

- Speaking and signing:
  Focus on the main points
- Listening:
  Sustain concentration
  Remember specific points
  Listen to other's reactions
- Group discussion and interaction:
  Take turns in speaking
  Relate their contributions to what has gone before
  Valuing others' contributions
- Drama:
  Use language and actions to explore ... situations, characters and emotions
  Role play

A non-verbal interview

Learners with little or no verbal vocabulary can engage in this activity, focusing on the concepts of turn taking and question and answer as in a verbal interview. Through intensive interaction (see Chapter 3), the learner has the opportunity to take the lead ('ask a question'), by vocalising, gesturing, or moving. The person supporting the learning process then responds ('answers a question'). Replying to a response that is not formal language and is possibly pre-intentional is a key stage to motivating responses. At a later stage, this process can be reversed to see how the learner 'answers'.

Reading

One of the prerequisites for learning to read is that the learner is able to 'focus on people, objects and patterns' (Equals 1999a).

The key elements of reading as laid out in the National Curriculum stress the importance of learners using 'a range of strategies to make sense of what they read'.

Before we can expect learners to recognise and read words it is necessary to develop, through experience and practice, the concept of what a word is and then a visual awareness of print. For some learners 'reading' will involve signs, symbols, Braille or pictures rather than print. The strategies used can incorporate the interpretation and understanding of a variety of signs or signing systems. Pictures or pictorial representations can be 'read' as well. The first steps include differentiating, matching, sorting and naming objects (Figure 8.2).

Greg's case

Greg expresses his choices by reaching out towards the object he has chosen. When offered a small number of hand-held instruments, Greg usually chooses a tambourine as he enjoys the sound it makes. Greg was differentiating by experience and by recognition of the circular shape of the tambourine. In order to extend Greg's differentiation skills, he was offered a variety of tambourines of varying colours, size and shape. Greg continued to choose the tambourine with which he was familiar. This option was temporarily removed in order to encourage Greg to select an instrument using more sophisticated criteria. Staff recorded his choices, noting the colour, shape and position of the tambourine chosen (this explored the possibility that Greg was choosing an instrument because it was easier for him to reach). Greg soon began to show a preference for a black, star shaped tambourine. Now when the two tambourines are offered along with other instruments, Greg can immediately differentiate between the two and make an informed choice over which one to play.

Using symbols

For most people who are able to read, the use of symbols is concerned with communicating ideas very quickly and simply. For people with severe learning difficulties, they may provide the only means whereby meaning can be communicated in printed form.

(Detheridge and Detheridge 1997).

The Makaton signing system uses signs to highlight key words and to focus on the meaning of these words when they are

83

The first stages; some examples	Example task
• differentiation	choosing round objects from a choice of shapes
• matching (shape/colour)	finding an identical object from a choice
• sorting	cutlery, cups, plates through eye pointing
• naming	gesturing towards/looking at a named object

Figure 8.2   Pre-reading skills

being spoken. The matching symbols can be used to build meaningful sentences that can then be read back. The first step is to work on matching symbols with their meanings.

Ian's case

Ian is able to give brief descriptions of recent events. After a trip to the shops he was able to say, 'I went to the shops' and use the Makaton signs for the key words, 'I', 'went' and 'shops'. By using the Makaton signs he has already started to break the sentence down into units of meaning. Ian is asked to find the symbols for each of these key words from a selection of six cards. Once he has identified the three symbols he is asked to sequence them and finally read back his sentence.

Linking a symbol to its meaning can be a difficult process and the activity may need to be repeated many times, in different contexts, before a learner can independently identify the correct symbol for a word. The above case shows Ian recognising and reading symbols from his direct experience. The next stage is to use symbols in a more abstract way and for gathering information.

The shopping list in Figure 8.3 shows how symbols can be used to write a list clearly.

milk   bread   biscuits   cheese

Figure 8.3   Shopping list symbols (symbols available through Widgit Software Ltd, see Useful addresses)

> **Information**
>
> *Literacy Through Symbols* (Detheridge and Detheridge 1997) has many good examples of using symbols for lists and instructions.

It is a good idea to have a collection of core Makaton vocabulary that is used consistently and to have the symbols displayed with the corresponding word clearly beneath it. This can then be used as a bank of words for word recognition work. Each learner can begin to build up a vocabulary that is of personal relevance to him or her.

As well as Makaton there are a number of other pictorial symbol systems available. These include: Rebus, PCS (Picture Communication Symbols), Compics and Sigsymbols from Widgit Software Ltd (see Useful addresses).

Using pictures

Ideas for picture resources:

- magazines;
- computer clip art discs;
- 'Colour Cards' produce box sets with categories such as home, sport and leisure and food;
- food packaging can be useful – see Chapter 7 for more information.

It is important that any pictures used as a teaching resource display the subject only, on a clear background. For example, if you require a picture of a bag, make sure it is not being held by anyone as this gives unnecessary pictorial information and can lead to misunderstanding.

Writing

Writing is used to communicate meaning and ideas to a reader. It is not necessary to be able to hold or manipulate a pen in order to do this.

The writing segment consists of the following elements:

- Communicating meaning:
  Use of a variety of methods including pictures, symbols,

drawing and eye pointing to communicate meaning/ needs to others.

- Fine motor skills:
  Development of skills to manipulate picture cards, computer or writing implements. Pointing with hand or finger.
- Writing familiar words:
  Write words in a meaningful context, e.g. own name on a form, items on a shopping list.

Amy's case

Amy is excellent at making eye contact. She has very little head or arm movement. She has learned to recognise many symbols through consistent use of them during her sessions at college. Amy is able to build up sequences by eye pointing towards the symbol she wants to choose. In this way she writes immediately relevant sentences and makes her meaning known to anyone who can read the symbols.

Many learners benefit from the option of choosing symbols and writing sentences via the computer keyboard or overlay. 'Symwrite 2000' and 'Writing With Symbols' (Widgit Software Ltd) are good examples of symbol writing software (see Useful addresses at the back of this book).

If it is appropriate for the learner to work towards more formal writing, it will be necessary to start by learning to hold and manipulate writing tools. If the learner is unable to grasp a tool independently, he or she may need hand-over-hand support, or be willing to initiate contact by reaching out towards a keyboard or communication board (see Chapter 3 for further information on acceptance of touch). Exercises to practise increased control may start with guiding a pen, pencil, mouse or another object the learner can manipulate along the edge of a raised shape from left to right. Initially this may need to be done with hand-over-hand assistance. The aim here is for the learner to independently and consistently move the tool along the edge.

It may be relevant to continue by teaching a learner to trace or copy over their name, as this is personal and has practical use in their life. Equals (1999a) provides a very useful breakdown for copy writing. It suggests starting by showing the learner a photograph of himself or herself and saying 'This is you' and then showing a name card and saying, 'This is your name.' The learner's name is then written clearly and the learner is asked to copy the letters of their name underneath.

'(Learners) who have poor fine motor skills or coordination may have considerable difficulty in forming conventional letters and it may be that "drawing" as a form of writing provides them with a means of written communication' (Ackerman and Mount 1991).

Peter's case

Peter prefers to use a paintbrush with a built-up handle to develop his fine motor control. He is able to choose the colour of paint he wishes to use by moving the brush to the correct pot. Peter works on a large sheet of paper on a tilted board. He responds to requests to paint particular objects by repeating the word and moving the brush to the paper. Peter always begins independently, but the development of his fine motor skills benefits from some regular hand over hand assistance. He asks staff to stop when he feels he has had enough help. Peter also initiates his own paintings and enjoys having others guess what he is painting.

Drawings and paintings can be saved to make lists and sets of instructions, or can be collected together over time to form a diary. These can then be 'read' back at any time.

Time

The time segment consists of the following elements:

- Identifying single events:
  Recognising an event, activity or task by linking it to an object of reference.
- Sequencing events:
  Using a timetable. Putting events into order using objects of reference and symbols.
- Anticipating events:
  Repeated routines. Predicting what is going to happen and making choices.

Time is an abstract concept. It requires an understanding that events happen in a sequence. In addition, each event is made up of a sequence of smaller events. Time is used to record events that have happened and to predict future events.

Using objects of reference can be a useful way to introduce the concept of time.

William's case

William attends a weekly interpersonal skills course. He is not experienced at making choices and he becomes nervous and distressed without a clear structure. His session consists of a choice of activities within three distinct parts: music, exercise/ massage, and refreshment. For a while, the structure of the session remains the same each week providing continuity and promoting anticipation of the next activity. At the beginning of the session William is offered the object of reference for music and initially guided to the circle of chairs where this activity will take place. William is also given the appropriate object of reference before moving on to each of the other activities. Once William has linked each activity with an object of reference he will be more prepared for these activities in a different order or in a different context. William's next step will be to use the objects to choose activities.

Objects of reference can also be used to represent a timetable of events. They can be placed in a tray or a similar container that is split into sections. The tray should have a number of compartments, one for each of the relevant objects of reference. Each time that the group is moving on to the next activity, the whole tray is shown, picking up the objects which represent the activities already completed, until the next activity's object is reached. This can help learners to anticipate events and make choices (see Chapter 4 for examples of objects of reference).

The planned activities for the morning may also be represented pictorially, or by using symbols that the learner is familiar with. If appropriate, these can be accompanied by clock faces showing the times at which these activities are going to take place. Learners can input into planning by picking and arranging pictures and symbols. The Makaton sign, 'later' can be used to reassure a learner that an anticipated event will happen.

Being able to predict and influence what is going to happen is often reassuring to the learner, and is working towards the learner taking control and making choices. See Tamsin's case opposite

Tamsin's case

Tamsin enjoys her day at college and takes part enthusiastically in a wide range of activities. Her behaviour indicates a need for a clear structure to her sessions. At the beginning of each session she attends, Tamsin fills in a learning agreement which lists the activities she plans to cover in the session. The document serves several purposes for her, but in the context of time, it provides her with a clear structure of the session ahead. It allows her to consider these activities in advance, aiding smooth transition from one activity to another. It gives her control over planning her learning.

Number

In order to begin to count, the learner has to realise that different objects or people are separate entities. Practical tasks, such as ensuring that each person in the group has a cup or a plate relies on the learner recognising that each person is a separate being, thus requiring a separate cup or plate.

There are several counting games in which learners can match either the colour or shape, or the number. These activities do not rely on the learner understanding or recognising a number. Some examples are: dominoes – tactile, shape or number; bingo; Whot! by Waddingtons.

Some learners may prefer more physical games such as throwing beanbags onto numbered targets or playing skittles. Such activities can be extended, with a member of the group being responsible for keeping the score on a sheet of paper or computer or abacus or with cubes.

By sitting in a circle, several concepts of number and space can be taught while passing a ball, or naming people. Below are some examples of these concepts:

- next to
- opposite
- left/right
- two along
- clockwise/anti-clockwise
- between

The learning opportunities discussed in this chapter are designed to develop the language and mathematical concepts of the learner. To enable the learner to foster an understanding of these concepts the activities should be short, frequent and repetitive, with variation depending on the particular needs of the individual. The activities should be carefully planned for specific sessions. However, opportunities to reinforce this learning may occur at any time; at home, at work, in other subject areas (refer to the core subjects web in Chapter 3). Everyone involved in the care and education of a learner needs to be aware of the current learning goals and the range of ways in which they can support them.

Chapter 9

Physical education

The aim of physical education is to enable learners to use, understand and extend their physical abilities.

As in all areas of the framework, it is essential from the start to focus on establishing relationships and finding out about the learner's likes and dislikes (refer to the foundation skills in Chapter 3).

Introduction

This chapter begins by outlining the structure of the physical education subject area and explaining the aims of the additional studies. The scope of this chapter includes three of the six segments of the physical education subject wheel shown in Figure 9.1: body awareness, assisted movement and negotiating obstacles. The segments are described through case studies, activity examples, objective setting, recording examples and equipment ideas. This chapter concludes by looking at links between physical education and other courses and general life skills.

The structure of the physical education course

The elements within physical education, shown as segments in the subject wheel, are identified in Key Stages 1 and 2 of the National Curriculum, 'to be physically active; to adopt the best possible posture and the appropriate use of the body; to engage in activities that develop cardiovascular health, flexibility, muscular strength and endurance . . .' (Department For Education 1995).

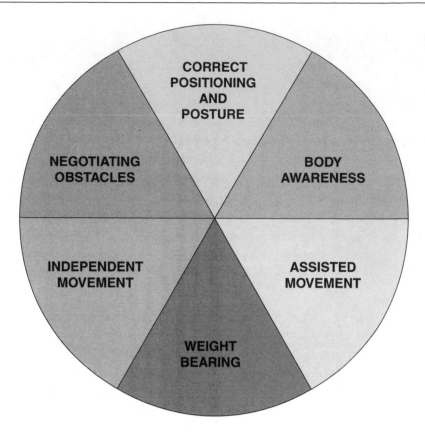

Figure 9.1 Subject wheel

Progression between segments

Some of the segments in the physical education subject wheel can be thought of as progressive steps along a continuum. Miller (1998) states that, 'Two aspects are particularly important to consider: firstly, positioning which is an essential prerequisite for optimum functional ability; secondly, independent mobility, which opens up a whole range of opportunities to a person with PMLD' (profound and multiple learning difficulties). The fundamental part of the subject wheel, correct positioning and posture, facilitates optimum assisted movement and weight bearing. Assisted movement is a building block towards independent movement which, in turn, leads to the most advanced skill area, negotiating obstacles. Body awareness complements and may be developed through all of the other areas. The remaining segments are defined as follows:

- Correct positioning and posture:
  Adopting and/or maintaining a body posture that enhances (and/or lessens the deterioration of) comfort, movement, spatial orientation, sensory awareness and accessibility to facilities.

- Weight bearing:
  Maintaining full support of the body through the limbs with minimal support from another person and/or equipment as necessary. Weight-bearing facilitates improved posture, circulation and mobility, builds strength and is a step towards independent movement.
- Independent movement:
  Whole or part body movement without physical assistance from another person. Learners may use equipment, the environment and verbal, signed or gestural encouragement to achieve this. Such movement increases confidence, self-esteem, enhances circulation, balance, strength and stamina.

Additional studies

There are five additional studies courses within the physical education subject area which have strong links with the physical education subject wheel. The content of the additional studies courses overlaps with the main subject wheel. The additional studies courses share many of the same elements as physical education as well as containing some different segments such as:

- self-care skills;
- environmental awareness;
- concentration;
- memory and anticipation.

Additional studies consist of the following:

Water-based physical education
To enable learners to use, understand and extend their physical abilities, gain confidence and control in the water and develop self-care skills.

Community-based swimming
To enable learners to use, understand and extend their physical abilities, increase independence and access community facilities.

Outdoor pursuits
To enable learners to use, understand and extend their physical abilities, negotiate obstacles and develop an awareness of outdoor environments.

Sequenced movement programmes
To enable learners to use, understand and extend their physical abilities, build relationships and develop concentration, memory and anticipation.

Wheelchair mobility
To enable learners to develop skills in using manual and electric wheelchairs with an emphasis on confidence, independence and safety.

Body awareness

Body awareness can be defined as an understanding of the names and functions of the different parts of the body, their relationship to other parts of the body and the body as a whole.

Activity examples:

Below are four activities designed to develop body awareness skills. There are a variety of tasks within for each activity as, 'We all have different abilities, interests and needs and these must be catered for individually' (Pointer 1993).

Music, movement and drama
- Daniel touching Sarah's arm and singing 'Daniel touches Sarah's arm . . .' to music as part of a greetings activity.
- Swirling of stick with streamers to music.
- Waving and lifting of parachute to different volume and tempo of music.

Body Awareness, Contact and Communication programme (Knill and Knill 1986)
- Saying keywords such as 'head' or 'hand' when using or touching a body part.
- Assisted movement to demonstrate functions of body parts.
- Anticipating and initiating movement of body parts in the programme sequence.

'My Body' projects
- Games that concentrate on developing the use of one particular body part (e.g. adapted floor skittles for grasp and release of ball, knocking soft-play blocks over by kicking a beach ball to develop use of legs and feet).
- Drawing around hands and feet. Making a collage by cutting out and decorating the hand and foot shapes.

- Identifying people in the group from photographs or shadows.

Dressing and self-care
- experiencing a running commentary with key words such as 'head', 'arm' and 'leg' whilst dressing with assistance.
- copying gestures showing how and where to don items of clothing.
- shopping for clothing, focusing on size and function of clothes.

'Considering the nature of the relationships between staff and learners may be seen as the first priority in establishing a positive climate for learning' (Sebba *et al.* 1993).

Recording example

Kate's case

Kate enjoys interacting with staff. She likes to look smart and particularly enjoys wearing nail varnish. Kate has profound and complex learning difficulties. She has very limited movement in each limb. Kate worked on an adapted Body Awareness, Contact and Communication programme (Knill and Knill 1986). This was followed by a hand massage and ended in her favourite activity, varnishing her nails. Kate achieved her objectives which were to increase body awareness and to build relationships. Her motivation to participate in varnishing her nails helped her to achieve increased movement in her hands, by holding her usually clenched hand open. Her developing body awareness was reflected in the change from showing an interest in the tasks to consistently initiating movement of her arm or leg after hearing the keyword 'arm' or 'leg' (even if the sequence of movements was altered). Kate built a trusting relationship with Julia through their joint involvement in the task, Kate's attentiveness was recorded as progressing from 'some of the time' to 'all of the time' for parts of the interaction.

Kate's progress was recorded during the activity, after each movement. Staff involved Kate by reading aloud and observing her responses as they completed the form shown in Figure 9.2.

Learner .... Staff .... Date .... Place .... Time ....

Activity	Participation						Attentiveness				Comments
	P	I	R	E	C	I	n	s	m	a	
wiggle fingers		/						/			
rotate wrists			/					/			
bend and straighten arms					/				/		

P = Passivity, I = Interest, R = Recognition, E = Expectation, C = Cooperation, I = Initiation, n = none of the time, s = some of the time, m = most of the time, a = all of the time

Figure 9.2   'Body Awareness, Contact and Communication' activity programme (adapted from Knill 1986)

Assisted movement

Assisted movement can be defined as whole body or part body movement that results from cooperation and an effort to move independently. Support, direction and encouragement from another person and/or the use of equipment or the environment can also be used.

Activity examples:

Pointer (1993) states, 'One question that is often asked when organising a sporting, recreational or movement opportunity for people with challenging physical and learning needs is "what do I do?" A small, varied selection of activities and tasks to develop assisted movement skills is provided below:

Group games
- grasping, placing and releasing a ball down a tube (with assistance if required) to play an adapted floor skittles game;
- holding (with assistance if required) and releasing a ball attached by elastic cord to the ceiling to knock down skittles;
- stretching arms (with assistance if required) to push a beach ball across a table in a game of tabletop volleyball.

Self-care
- opening hand and holding hand flat to apply nail varnish;
- pouring and rubbing hand cream on to hands (assistance to pour correct amount and rub in all of the cream may be required);

- bending ankles and pushing feet into shoes (with assistance to hold shoes steady if required).

Greetings and musical interaction
- greeting by stretching out an arm or leg to touch another learner or staff (with assistance if required);
- beating a tambourine with a hand in slow time to a 'hello' song (with assistance if required);
- holding and playing a musical instrument e.g. an afuche (a hand held wooden circle covered in metal beaded material) with assistance if required. Coordination can be developed by playing an afuche, as the handle is held with one hand and the beads are rubbed by the other hand.

An objective setting case study

It is important that a learner's individual objective is:

- negotiated with the learner in whatever way suits the learner;
- useful for the learner's daily life;
- within the physical abilities of the learner;
- motivating for the learner;
- challenging for the learner.

Imran's case

Imran enjoys eating and preparing food and always participates in activities related to food. He has some movement in his arms but often requires assistance for fine motor tasks. One of Imran's individual objectives was to reach out and touch a switch (with assistance if required but with an emphasis on independent initiation). A high sensitivity switch was used. It operated a whisk to make a lemon mousse which Imran particularly enjoys eating. After three months Imran had progressed from requiring assistance to requiring only occasional physical prompts (a light tap on the elbow) to initiate the movement and place his hand on the switch.

Negotiating obstacles

Negotiating obstacles can be defined as using independent movement combined with exploration, cause and effect and problem solving to overcome new problems encountered when a desired route is obstructed.

Activity examples:

Countryside walking
- walking over rough, uneven and sloping ground;
- climbing over obstacles such as fallen logs;
- negotiating stiles;
- choosing which route to take to avoid impassable obstacles or terrain.

Obstacle course
- steering a wheelchair between obstacles;
- bending under a horizontal pole;
- rolling a large beach ball out of the way;
- stepping from inside one hoop to another;
- climbing up an inclined balance bench and over a trestle.

Journeys and excursions
- boarding and alighting from cars, buses and trains;
- stepping up and down kerbs;
- using stairs and escalators;
- negotiating turnstiles and ticket barriers.

Trim trail (obstacle course)
- stepping over hurdles;
- walking along balance beams;
- climbing over climbing fence;
- hanging on to monkey bars;
- pulling up on chin-up bars.

Examples of individual learner objectives:
- To push a trolley from the kitchen to the living room (with assistance through doorways if required).
- To walk over rough, level terrain with verbal prompts and pointing.
- To board and alight from a bus with only verbal and physical prompts.
- To negotiate a woodland trail (with uneven ground and partially obstructing vegetation) with only verbal, gestural and physical prompts.
- To complete the (trim trail) balance bars obstacle with prompting and physical assistance from one member of staff.
- To complete the trim trail independently.

Equipment

A trim trail is an extremely useful resource to develop negotiating obstacle skills for learners who can walk independently. Trim trails consist of obstacles such as hurdles (for stepping over), balance bars (to walk along) and climbing fences (to climb over). These obstacles vary in difficulty and can be adapted to suit individual learner's abilities. Balance bars, for instance, can be used to develop stepping skills as well as demanding balance skills. Using a trim trail in a local park or recreation area offers learners opportunities to extend their use of community facilities.

Indoors, an obstacle course can be created without much specialist equipment:

- climbing over an obstacle: balance bench, trestle and crash mat, or balance bench and wall rail, or steps;
- stepping over an obstacle: hoops, or balance bench;
- bending under an obstacle: two stands, lath (metal bars), lath with hanging threads attached;
- crawling under an obstacle: two balance benches, parachute.

This chapter concludes by outlining the place of physical education within the learning framework as a whole and other aspects of learners' lives. 'A well organised curriculum ... clarifies the concepts of teachers about the purpose of their teaching' (Brennan 1985). In addition, learners' progress is enhanced by the fact that skills learned in one subject area are transferable to other areas. The core subject web (Chapter 3) illustrates the links between physical education and other courses. To expand on this:

Wider links

- Body awareness is a facet of awareness of self and others which is a foundation skill at the centre of the web.
- Purposeful movement and exercise and health issues link physical education to life skills.
- Negotiating obstacles and problem solving links physical education to science and technology.

Aspects of the physical education subject area may be incorporated into other subject areas; leisure pursuits e.g. swimming, joining a gym; social activities e.g. fun run, disco; home life e.g. pushing a trolley; work e.g. reaching up to put books on shelves when working in a library. In all areas, it is important to identify the best physical postures from which a learner may gain maximum movement and, therefore, participation. However, a learner may be unable to achieve this maximum potential if they are tense. Building relationships between learners and others is a key component to ensuring that the learner is able to communicate needs and feel comfortable and secure.

Figure 9.3 shows examples of ways in which learners can benefit from physical education in many other aspects of their lives.

Physical Benefits	Cognitive/Personal Benefits	Lifestyle Benefits
purposeful movement	enjoyment	social interaction
hand–eye coordination	sense of achievement	build relationships
strength	builds confidence	teamwork skills
suppleness	opportunity to compete	develop personal interests
stamina	relieve stress	increase life experiences
weight control	provides opportunities for purposeful activity	appropriate channelling of stress
greater independence in movement	opportunities to develop body awareness	opportunities to access mainstream sports and leisure facilities
reduce effects of specific medical conditions	provides opportunities to explore	enhances adult status through participation in age appropriate activities
opportunities to develop acceptance of touch	provides opportunities to develop communication skills	
improved circulation (cardiovascular)	provides opportunities to develop interaction skills	
aids relaxation after exercise	greater awareness through increased oxygen to the brain	
increased awareness through sensory stimulation	builds self-esteem through improved personal presentation (e.g. posture, muscle tone, weight etc.)	

Figure 9.3   Links between physical education and other areas of learning

Chapter 10

Creative and cultural studies

This subject area aims to provide opportunities for expressive and interactive communication through a range of creative and cultural experiences.

As in all areas of the framework, it is essential from the start to focus on establishing relationships and finding out about the learner's likes and dislikes (refer to the foundation skills in Chapter 3).

Introduction

It is important for learners with profound and complex learning difficulties to have opportunities to contribute to the creation of multicultural ideas and activities in order to develop self-esteem, an awareness of others, self-expression, motivation and increased participation. It has been said that 'the arts are a powerful means of exploring and communicating ideas and feelings and of understanding and appreciating our common and different cultures' (Knight 2000).

The creative and cultural studies subject area has evolved from the changing needs and experiences of both learners and staff over several years and this is a process which continues.

This chapter expands on the subject wheel in Figure 10.1 and includes approaches to the sharing of knowledge and experience across subject areas and with other agencies. Approaches include: use of themes, developing schemes of work, their delivery and evaluation. The chapter includes examples of partnership projects with local schools, mainstream colleges, churches, community theatres and professional bodies.

The creative and cultural studies subject area provides a flexible structure upon which to build and develop ideas, activities and materials. It aims to offer opportunities to

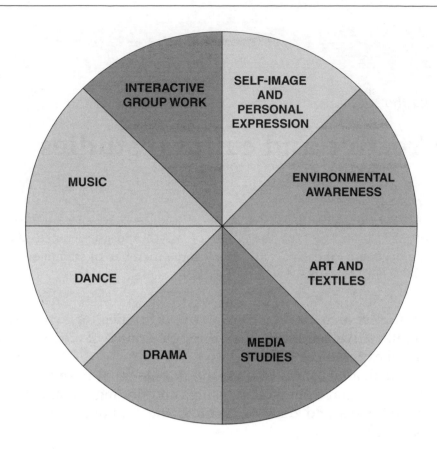

Figure 10.1 Subject wheel

motivate learners who require dynamic approaches to both familiar and new activities. The challenge is to look at the equipment and materials available and to work imaginatively with them. 'In some ways creativity can be defined as a search for alternatives. This is especially true when you set out to be creative about something that already exists' (De Bono 1995).

Within this context, people can provide a wealth of innovative and immediate resources. We all have skills and experiences to use when planning and executing activities. However, 'when asked to be "creative"' many of us automatically think of art-related activities such as painting and drawing. Our own memories of success and failure will have a bearing on how we, as professionals, may approach this area of "being creative". Personal reluctance to experience new areas and approaches may lessen the opportunities of those we work with' (Hutchinson 2001). As practitioners, we need to set aside the idea that we are 'no good' at, for example, art or music. There are no mistakes to be made by either the learner or the facilitator, and no pieces of 'bad' work. Each mark on the paper, each vocalisation, facial expression or body movement represents an achievement deserving of acknowledgement.

Jenny's case

Jenny is an inquisitive and cheerful young lady who enjoys engaging people she knows well in conversation. When Jenny first began at College she found it difficult to accept her own successes. This was partly due to her autism and her low self-expectations. During art-based activities, Jenny was encouraged to create independent pieces of work. However, each time she successfully completed a drawing or painting and her success was acknowledged, Jenny destroyed her work. Jenny was encouraged to accept her work as something of worth and importance. At the beginning of each activity, Jenny and a member of staff filled in a 'learning agreement' which they both signed. The focus of the agreement was to encourage Jenny to 'try' to complete a piece of work to take home. Each piece of work was laminated and accompanied by a photocopy of the agreement. Jenny also began to get positive feedback from her parents about her work. Gradually, Jenny became more confident in her work and began to take pride in it, choosing to share it with others.

Jenny has responded positively to working within a negotiable structure which has enabled her to develop and initiate coping strategies.

Being creative is also about solving problems, experimenting with ideas and taking risks. The uncertainty that accompanies this puts both the learners and staff into situations that make them feel vulnerable, apprehensive and unsure as to what is expected of them. Working within a structure often helps to alleviate some of these anxieties. Themes, as shown in Figure 10.2, can provide a useful foundation upon which to build a series of activities that explore creative and cultural experiences.

Learning to operate a camera enabled Peter to build confidence in his interpersonal skills and develop interactions with his peers.

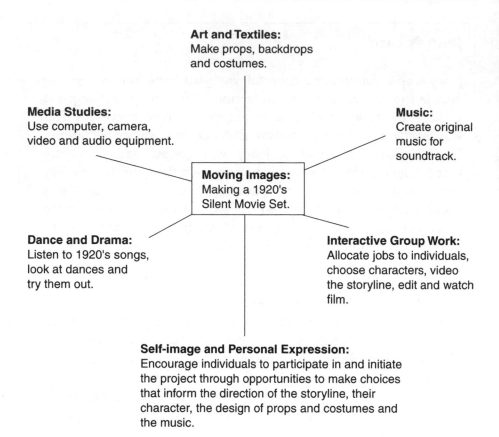

Figure 10.2 Example of a theme

Peter's case

Peter is a shy individual who is apprehensive when in company. He has profound and complex learning difficulties and uses a wheelchair. Peter is able to manoeuvre his wheelchair independently. Peter initially found working in a group difficult and chose to watch the group from across the room. With the introduction of the video camera and monitor, Peter began to focus on individuals in the group, bringing them closer via the camera which he operated independently. By the end of the project, Peter was successfully participating in activities alongside members of the group.

Additional activity ideas

Each segment of the creative and cultural studies subject wheel includes a range of activities that can be used independently or within a theme-based structure. The examples below may also be linked into other subject areas (refer to the core subjects web in Chapter 3).

Self-image and personal expression:

- using a mirror, photograph or touch to develop awareness of self;
- looking at the individual: height, colour of eyes, hair, skin tone, vocalisations;
- making informed choices about appearance.

Art and textiles:

- investigate light, dark and movement using an overhead projector and screen;
- create a variety of environments: forest, underwater, seasons, cave;
- listen to environmental sounds, create musical and vocal sounds;
- experience a range of art techniques and materials: pencil, pastel, paint, clay, composite work; collage, model making;
- weave tactile pictures, use material to make soft sculptures.

Media studies:

- use a video camera to produce a diary of a day or week;
- produce sound effects for film work;
- poster making: involve choice making, research and presentation skills;
- use a computer with adapted switches to develop creative writing using words, symbols and pictures.

Drama:

- explore emotions and feelings through: discussion, verbal/facial expression, Makaton, pictures, music, masks and characters;
- warm-up exercises: nod head, shrug shoulders, lift arms, tap knees, stamp feet;
- adapt poems and traditional stories or write your own: act out;
- use an overhead projector and white sheet to create a shadow screen: explore a story in silhouette.

Dance:

- explore spatial awareness: movements: linear, circular and random;
- look at different dance forms: Chinese Lion dance, flamenco, ballroom;
- projects: link movement and dance with musical and dramatic presentations;
- use massage to develop acceptance of touch;
- use a sequence of gentle movements as a warm up exercise.

Music:

- explore rhythm through turn-taking, echoing, hands, voices and instruments;
- develop an appreciation of a range of musical styles from all cultures;
- create and perform original pieces of music: look at beginnings and ends, tempo, volume and intensity.

Themes activities which interlink across the framework can provide a diverse resource base. One object (see Figure 10.3) can become a multifaceted project leading to a range of investigations, problem-solving situations and sensory experiences.

> *the different purposes played by sensory experiences in the arts and in the sciences should be explicitly drawn out ... handling different kinds of materials may form a part of a science activity. In contrast, observing them closely, looking at line, texture, colour, imagining their history or future through play or fantasy may form part of an arts activity.*

(Craft 1999)

Planning and practical applications

Introducing and executing theme-based activities involves discussion, research and delegation prior to delivery. It is important to choose a theme which reflects the needs and interests of the learners and to use appropriate equipment and materials.

Suggested guidelines:

- organise a team meeting;
- collect background information about the group and their needs and preferences;

**ART AND TEXTILES:
PRINTING:**

- Cut apple into quarters/halves – print sequences of patterns
- Roll apple across paper to create a pattern using different colours
- Print onto paper, material and wood
- To explore texture of apple

**COOKING:
BAKED APPLES:**

- Prepare apple
- Fill apple with dried fruit
- Cook apple
- Explore tastes – apple – raw/cooked, fruit – sultanas, sugar, syrup
- Safety and hygiene

THEME:

TAKE AN APPLE

**THE ENVIRONMENT:
GROWING PLANTS:**

- Cut apple in half, look at the position of the seeds
- Remove the seeds
- Fill a flower-pot with compost, plant seeds
- Water seeds
- Observe and record growth

**COMMUNITY LIVING:
SHOPPING SKILLS:**

- Write a shopping list
- Recognise an apple
- Match with picture
- Choose an apple
- Use a shopping basket
- Queue and pay for apple
- Put apple into shopping bag

Figure 10.3   Developing theme-based activities across the framework
(Hutchinson 2001)

- select a theme: include suggestions from learners;
- delegate areas of work to individuals – involve staff and learners;
- research theme: books, magazines, libraries, people, CD-ROM, Internet;
- complete a project outline;
- collect materials: local scrap projects, companies, catalogues;
- list equipment required: electrical equipment, specialist materials;
- risk assessment: cables on floor, equipment needing supervision.

Scheme of work

This may take the form of a group project set over a block of time with opportunities for individual and group contributions. An example project concerned with different countries is displayed in Figure 10.4.

An activity plan may be used to specify the project outline in more detail by breaking elements down into steps, as shown in Figure 10.5.

Delivery

Before starting an activity it is important to look at the space available and ways in which it may need to be changed to enable individuals to participate. The following list outlines some areas which need to be considered before and during an activity:

- room layout: draw a floor plan;
- learner/staff ratios: may change with the needs of the group;
- equipment and materials: make a list of what is needed;
- positioning of learners and activities: for optimum access;

India	Week 1: • locate on map • Holi – spring festival	Week 2: • food – spicy potatoes • clothes
America	Week 3: • locate on map • famous landmarks	Week 4: • food – hamburgers • Hollywood
Egypt	Week 5: • locate on map • language – Arabic	Week 6: • history – pyramids • animals – camels
Brazil	Week 7: • locate on map • listen to music	Week 8: • food – coffee • houses – colour/shape

Figure 10.4   A project outline: looking at different countries

TIME	CONTENT	ACTIVITY AIMS	EQUIPMENT
10.00	Project work • find India on the map • Holi spring festival – look at the colours used in the festival – throw confetti over each other, listen to the stories linked to the festival and pass pictures around the group	To encourage participation in group activities To develop a greater understanding of where we live To make choices	Map of world, festivals book, confetti, selection of coloured paper, pictures of festival

Figure 10.5 Example of an activity plan

- staff facilitating different sections: discuss with individuals;
- learners to lead parts of session: consider structures which best allow learners to take the lead (refer to Chapter 4);
- communication – objects of reference, Makaton, symbols and pictures;
- teaching approaches: individual, pair and group work, interactive, objectives led etc. (refer to Chapter 3).

Evaluation

Evaluating a theme or activity will highlight achievements and contributions made by individuals and inform staff of any changes needed for future activities. (See Figure 10.6 for an evaluation format.)

The list above provides a checklist for use both before and after activities. For example: were the learners positioned appropriately? Were there opportunities for individuals to lead parts of the activity? Were the correct materials and equipment used? An evaluation may take place at the end of each step of an activity as well as on completion. Opportunities for learners to contribute to the evaluation process need to be offered in ways that are accessible and meaningful to each individual (refer to Chapter 2).

ACTIVITY: India – Festival of Holi	OBSERVATIONS
Strengths:	Good participation by all members of the group – looking at different colours. Throwing confetti was good for encouraging eye-contact and visual tracking. Staff worked well as a team in responding to a change of direction when (learner) Jack took the initiative.
Weaknesses:	Needed colour in a textured or 3D format, not just smooth paper. Layout needs to be less cluttered for learners with visual impairment to negotiate safely.
Opportunities for learner-to-learner interaction:	Each person was encouraged to pass the coloured paper to the person next to them during the festival ritual part. This was achieved by everyone either independently or with help. Katy helped Sam (both learners) by taking his hand and directing it towards the table.
Opportunities for learners to evaluate activity:	Individuals encouraged to contribute through reflective discussion, facial expression, vocalisation, objects of reference and written work. Recorded.
Any changes to be made for next activity?	Recap colour exploration using a range of coloured textures and objects.

Figure 10.6   Example of an evaluation of an activity

Partnership projects

Establishing links with local organisations e.g. local schools, professional bodies and community theatres can provide opportunities for learners with profound and complex learning difficulties to participate in community-based activities and settings. Figure 10.7 is an example of a partnership project plan.

Joint projects create shared experiences which encourage an awareness of others and their needs. Joint projects can also enable individuals (both those with learning difficulties and those without learning difficulties) to interact with greater confidence with each other. Good communication and support for all learners and staff is essential to ensure positive outcomes.

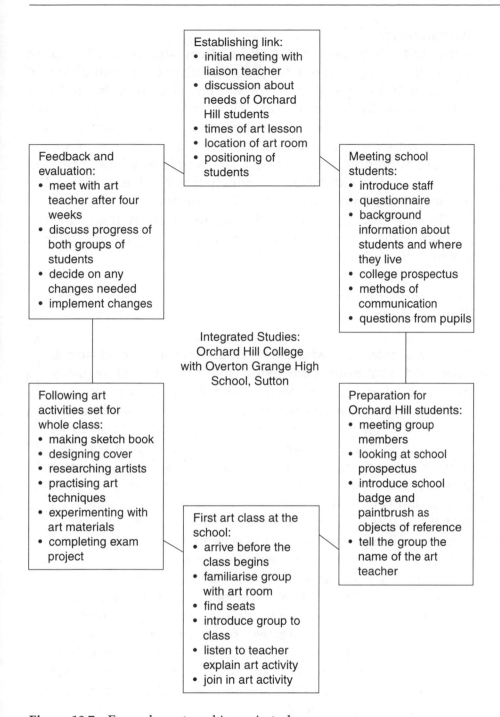

Figure 10.7   Example partnership project plan

Joint exhibitions in community settings

Exhibitions of art work produced collaboratively and presented in community settings provide opportunities to raise awareness and provide information to facilitate inclusion.

Joint Initiative

Four students from Orchard Hill College and an art class from Carshalton High School for boys produced an exhibition of works linked to a 'Carnival' theme. The class was divided into four groups. Each group was asked to create a carnival float based on a wheelchair. Sketches and photographs of each project were mounted and exhibited in the coffee bar of a local theatre. Invitations were sent out for people to attend a private viewing of the exhibition at which the head teacher of the school presented certificates to all exhibitors.

The enthusiasm, hard work and team effort made by the learners in this joint venture were acknowledged and shared through the exhibition.

Sylvia's case

Sylvia is a quiet lady who communicates through vocalisations, touch and facial expressions. Sylvia is visually impaired, requiring assistance when walking around and a 'hands-guided' approach when participating in activities. Sylvia is one of the learners taking part in the integrated art session at a local school. Sylvia completes the same art work as the pupils, using texture and scented materials in place of pencils and paints. Sylvia anticipates classroom routines and readily explores art materials with her hands, with help. Sylvia is able to recognise members of the class and the teacher who has a distinctive Welsh accent. Sylvia has gained confidence in the school environment and now walks around parts of the art room independently.

Sylvia has become an established member of the group. Sylvia and the school students have developed a shared confidence in working together. The joint project with the school art department has been extremely successful for both sets of learners and staff. In this third year of the project, learners with profound learning difficulties are participating in the same art examination work as the other students, using adapted equipment and materials when required.

Enabling learners to take the lead

The Arts can provide a flexible structure which allows learners to contribute to and direct the content of an activity and 'unknown' situations to be explored. A performing arts project was developed by Orchard Hill College and the Music Therapy Service at Southwest London Community NHS Trust, with learners with profound and complex learning difficulties who attended both services. A theme was selected by representatives from both groups and a story outline written. On the day of the workshop the staff and learners were given the same amount of information concerning content and running of the day. Feelings of apprehension were expressed by staff who felt they needed a more definite structure to work with. It was explained that for the participants to truly 'lead' and 'direct' the workshop it was important for everyone to begin from the same point. This led to a sense of curiosity as to how the workshop would progress. The workshop was divided into three groups: Drama, Music and Art. Each group used the story to develop a dramatisation, musical and vocal accompaniment, scenery and props. The workshop culminated in a performance in front of a small audience.

Damian's case

Damian is an outgoing individual who requires time to take in information, process it and make a response. Damian also has an extremely loud voice and has often experienced people wanting to ask him to 'be quiet' in some settings. As a member of the drama group Damian became immediately involved in the story, requesting to be the main character and directing the rest of the group and staff. He also changed the story to incorporate his own ideas. His leadership was enhanced by his strong voice.

Damian was able to understand that the group were 'acting-out' a story, and bring his own interpretation to the performance.

The workshop offered all the participants and staff opportunities to make a contribution to the overall end production at their own pace and level. At the end of the day staff were asked to complete evaluations which reflected very different feelings to those at the beginning of the workshop.

Some examples of staff comments about the workshop
- 'lots of opportunities for 1:1 interactions, participants negotiating content';
- 'opportunities for individuals to contribute to whole event';
- 'it was good to have the freedom to improvise and contribute at any level and in any way because there was no set expectation';
- 'the participants were recognised for their efforts';

- 'I felt a bit lost initially, but the day formed its own structure as it went along';
- 'very clear expectations for participants within a loose structure with equal participation';
- 'it's a good opportunity for our two departments to work together, and the participants clearly enjoyed the day'.

Being included in a group as a valued contributor is important to the individual learner and to those sharing the situation. Each establishment or group of learners will have its own experiences and set of needs which make it unique.

The advantage of the structure for this area of the framework is that it offers direction without stifling creativity. As with all areas of the framework, the individual learner is the focus, and the content and approaches arc adapted to suit the individual and the setting. The creative and cultural studies subject area offers varied opportunities to develop experiences through learner centred approaches incorporating individual and cultural diversity. Aspects of the work may be easily transferred across the framework (see core subjects web at the end of Chapter 3) and within different settings e.g. home, college, work.

Chapter 11

An induction for learners with visual and/or hearing impairments

This subject area aims to develop skills essential to the individual, taking into account the specific nature of his/her sensory impairment. It is termed 'induction' because it was created to enable learners to access other subject areas and inclusive opportunities armed with the additional skills and confidence required to cope with sensory deficit.

As in all areas of the framework, it is essential from the start to focus on establishing relationships and finding out about the learner's likes and dislikes (refer to the foundation skills in Chapter 3).

Introduction

This chapter reviews some practical measures to help practitioners identify sensory loss. It offers examples of structures and teaching approaches designed to boost the skills and confidence of each learner.

The nine segments of the subject wheel (Figure 11.1), in addition to the foundation skills described in Chapter 3, form the framework for this subject area. This chapter is limited to consideration of aspects of residual vision and hearing, mobility and orientation and personal development (confidence and self-esteem), while the remaining elements of the wheel are considered in other chapters.

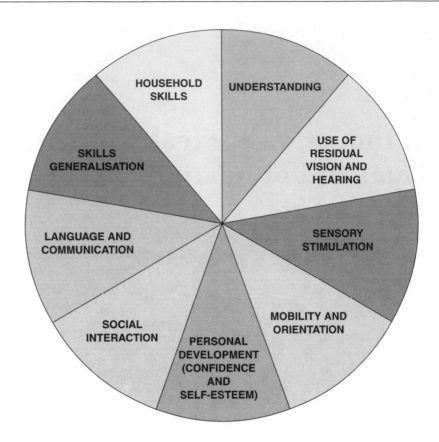

Figure 11.1 Subject wheel

Assessment Two elements of assessment are described in this section. Further guidance on assessment is located in Chapter 5. It should be remembered that relationship building (refer to Chapter 3) and assessment should be developed together. The emphasis is on finding out about each other, rather than staff 'doing' the assessing and learners 'being' assessed.

Information

Refer to *Baseline Assessment and Curriculum Target Setting* from Equals (1999a) (Tel: 0191 272 8600) for detailed learner assessments (see References).

Gathering information

The first step towards structuring learning for an individual, or group of individuals, is to find out about them. Information may be provided by the learner him/herself, by reading notes or reports from person-centred planning and by talking to other people who know the individual. However, it is important to note that information received may be inaccurate or incomplete. Some information can be checked by spending time with the learner engaged both in experiential assessments e.g. intensive interaction, interactive massage (refer to the Introduction and Chapter 3) and engaged in more formally structured skills assessments.

Grant's case

Grant has profound and complex learning difficulties. He is able to move his head and has limited movement in both arms. I was informed by several people that Grant was totally blind and showed little interest in anything. During a functional vision assessment, every time I switched on a coloured light to Grant's right, Grant turned his head towards the light and giggled.

The type of information required may vary according to individual circumstances and confidentiality issues. The checklist which follows identifies a few common priority areas:

- residual vision and hearing
- motivation (likes and dislikes)
- learning in other contexts (past and present)
- methods of communicating (including behaviours)
- relevant medical information
- care needs
- mobility
- relevant background information
- skills
- people, events.

Information

Refer to Helen Bradley's (1991) *Assessing Communication Together* from APLD (Tel: 01423 331404) for assessment approaches for learners with multi-sensory impairments (see References).

Functional vision and hearing assessments

The first step is to become familiar with the clues which may indicate a sensory loss. Many learners with profound learning difficulties are not referred to specialists either because the sensory loss is unnoticed, or because there is a lack of understanding of the ways in which examinations may be adapted (RNIB 1998). Informal observation can be carried out to establish whether it is possible that the learner may have a visual or hearing impairment, for example:-

Example clues (vision)
- appearance of eyes ('milky', eyes 'rove', ingrowing eyelashes);
- behaviours (eye poking, light gazing, unusual head movements, peers at people and objects);
- movement (collides with objects, anxious walking, better in some lighting conditions).

(RNIB Focus Factsheet 1992)

Example clues (hearing)
- appearance of ears (scarred, closed, discharging);
- speech/vocalisations (very loud or very quiet, monotonous);
- behaviour (bangs side of face, puts objects in ears, places fingers under ear lobes, poor balance);
- people (watches faces closely, avoids or flinches at loud noise).

(RNIB Focus Factsheet 1996)

If a sensory loss is suspected, the individual should be referred to the relevant specialist. This will provide a clinical assessment of the learner. However, an additional *functional* assessment is helpful for determining the best ways to work with the learner. It is important to remember that only 18 per cent of people classified as 'blind' have no sight, or light and dark perception only (Bruce *et al.* 1991).

Information

Functional vision and hearing assessment formats are available from the RNIB Certificate/Diploma course in Multiple Disability (Tel: 0121 643 9912).

Functional assessments are key tools in establishing teaching approaches for individuals and often provide critical information relating to the best ways to approach and communicate with learners.

Martina's case

Martina has severe learning difficulties and a visual impairment. Functional vision assessment indicated that Martina saw best in the lower part of her visual field. She was motivated by interaction with other people and used vocalisation and gesture to communicate. A learning objective was devised to enable Martina to sign 'hello' using 'h' from the Deaf Blind Manual Alphabet.

 This sign was carried out at Martina's waist level to make best use of her residual vision. Now, Martina initiates the sign and smiles. In this way, Martina is able to take control by signalling that she would like a person to greet her.

Learners may be encouraged to make optimum use of residual vision/hearing by experimenting with rewarding tasks and experiences involving use of these senses. Some examples are included in the session plan in the next section.

Planning and objectives

Following information gathering and individual assessment, provisional objectives and tasks may be planned for the individual and the group. These will form the basis of the initial learning structure, whether it takes place in college, at home, at work or elsewhere. The plans are 'provisional' because the individual learners will modify them, but a clear working structure is required from the outset so that learners and practitioners are able to function purposefully and confidently.

Creating individual objectives:

- Initially, a draft list of relevant individual objectives may be drawn from the information gathering and assessment. Some learners are able to influence the list at this stage, but many learners with profound learning difficulties will require actual experience of the suggested objectives in

119

order to understand the choices and communicate preference.

- The draft list should be amended to incorporate learner preferences. Each objective should then be made very specific and recording and teaching approaches defined. Further amendments may be required following evaluation.
- Some objectives may define practice rather than outcomes. For example, an objective for staff may be to engage in interactive massage with a learner and note any forms of communication offered by the learner. Other objectives may require a strongly structured approach (refer to example below), although it is critical to ensure that flexibility underpins all practice, such that a structured objective may be amended according to the learner's 'comments' or responses.

Figure 11.2 gives a record of achieving one individual objective.

Draft objective: Find his way independently.
Specific objective: Walk from study door to toilet door independently.
Teaching approach and recording:

Teaching Approach	Prompts Required	Comments
1. Bill, do you want to go to the toilet?		Speak on his right
2. Makaton sign toilet (hand-over-hand)		
3. Show object of reference (flannel)	HGT	Smiled
4. Place right hand on wall	HGT	
5. Track hand along wall	PP	Replaced hand on wall x 7
6. Locate flannel on toilet door	HGT	
7. Locate door handle	PP	

Prompts: HGT: hands guided through, PP: physical prompt, VP: verbal prompt

Figure 11.2   Example objective

Creating a plan:

A session plan is written to make sure everyone knows what to do, when and why. It also helps to ensure that the correct equipment is ready at the start. The plan should build in choices. But the plan is really only a way of thinking. Experienced practitioners are able to respond to learners flexibly and may deviate from the activities in the plan and yet still facilitate progress.

The individual objectives form the basis of the plan, but the learning time as a whole will require an overall structure i.e. Jon's objective to sign hello will be included in the plan under the 'greetings' section (refer to Figure 11.3).

- The plan should be based on evaluation comments of learners and staff from the previous session. In this way, everyone can have a 'say' in deciding the content.
- The plan should be used to reflect on how to improve the session and to think about the purpose of each activity. The framework or pattern of the plan may be used consistently over several weeks to enable learners to anticipate and make choices. However, the content, teaching approaches and expectations of progress should be changed or revisited every session.
- The framework or pattern of the plan may remain. However, individual learners should be able to influence this during the session. An example follows.

Chris' case

Chris is blind and partially deaf. He has profound learning difficulties and communication difficulties which are sometimes challenging. Chris is very clear about what he likes to do. He prefers 1:1 contact with certain people, he likes to give and receive foot massage and likes to have lots of drinks. Each of these activities were incorporated into our plan alongside the preferences of other members of the group. Over time, Chris was able to indicate choice by moving towards the area in which a preferred activity was offered.

The extract of a plan (Figure 11.3) includes individual objectives, communication focus points (CFP) and an overall structure or shape in addition to tasks/activities. An equipment list and floor plan will also be required.

Time	Content	Individual Objectives
9.45	Greetings Sit in close circle. Greet each person in turn using greetings sequence adapted to individual.	Frank: hold out hand to receive greeting. Susie: say hello and initiate hand contact.
CFP	Greetings sequence (refer to Chapter 4), adapt to individual.	
10.00	Getting to know you (relationship building): • hands-on-hands game: Make a pile of hands from everyone in the group taking a turn. • name game. Roll/pass a ball to someone saying/signing his/her name. • gather group round large drum. Tap a chant and name each person.	Jane: make contact with peers as well as staff. Susie: repeat names of people in group. Frank: extend hand towards others Mark: move hand slightly forwards to acknowledge contact. Jim: remain with group during each task.
CFP	Use objects of reference to choose tasks e.g. cooking (wooden spoon) or mat work (small mat). Present slowly and from best position for the individual's use of residual vision and hearing.	
10.15	Individual/group tasks • computer work • mat work e.g. interactive massage • cooking	Frank: use of vision to touch computer picture. Jim: work with another learner during cooking task.

CFP = communication focus points (Communication should be happening all the time but if working in a team, it is helpful to identify key moments when everyone has a clear remit to focus on it. It also provides a way of spelling out the structure and choices for learners.)

Figure 11.3   Example plan extract

Teaching approaches

A person with learning difficulties and additional sensory impairments requires learning support from people who spend time considering precisely which approaches are required. This section features some guidelines and examples for practitioners.

Checklist: supporting learners

- Slow down. It takes longer to process information with a sensory impairment.

- Approach slowly and use visual/sound warnings before making physical contact.
- Position yourself correctly. Remember which is his/her best side for hearing or seeing.
- Use clear speech in conjunction with other forms of communication appropriate to the individual e.g. signing, objects, pictures, symbols, gestures, smells, tactiles. Be consistent.
- Enable progress from a positive starting point – focus on the learner's likes and strengths.
- Build a positive working relationship together (refer to Chapter 3).
- Reinforce and celebrate every achievement, big or small.

Examples of teaching approaches for mobility and orientation

- *running commentary (accompanied by signing or other communication if required)*
  This technique is critical both for learners using wheelchairs and for those who walk. It enables learners to orientate and feel empowered. However, it is a skill which requires practice on the part of the practitioner. Example: 'Susie, we're at the shop. Susie, stop! Susie, reach out your hand for the door, please. Susie, well done. That's excellent. OK Susie, I'm guiding you into the shop...'

- *wheelchair routes and landmarks*
  If the person does not have verbal skills, it is difficult to communicate when they are feeling frightened because you are pushing the wheelchair too fast. It is important to move slowly and to explain the route using the running commentary technique, gestures and landmarks. Example: 'James, we are reaching the end of the path, (tap left shoulder) we're turning left. James reach out for the post (guides his hand to the post). Well done.'

- *environments*
  It is important to introduce the visually impaired learner to the environment by guiding him/her around the perimeter of the room and encouraging contact with the wall and key features. The layout should be as consistent as possible and any changes in the room should be introduced and explored. Use of good lighting and colour contrast can often help learners to see outline shapes, so door frames should be a different colour from walls and furniture should contrast with flooring. Plain colours are

easier to distinguish than busy patterns. The same practice should be applied in relation to tableware. A single, plain cup on a surface with contrasting colour may be much easier to visually locate than a patterned cup on a cluttered table with a patterned tablecloth.

- *guiding*
  Standard guiding techniques (RNIB 1995) do not always suit learners with profound learning difficulties. However, the basic principles are helpful and can be adapted to meet individual needs. Walking slowly and slightly ahead of the learner gives warning of changes in surface and obstacles. Holding your arm or hand, the learner can feel the movement of your body as you move aside or step up or down and they can also take control by altering the grasp on your arm to move you in front.

Examples of teaching approaches for developing the use of hearing

- talk to the learner as well as using signs, objects, pictures and other clues. For example say, 'Hello Sophie'. Then say it again and sign it, 'Hello Sophie'. In this way, Sophie uses her hearing first rather than relying solely on visual or tactile clues.
- minimise background noise. Echoes or constant and numerous sounds and talking can be very confusing. It can be hard to listen to speech and other sound cues if the TV or radio are on in the background. The learner should be encouraged to operate the TV and music system controls. Adapted switches may be required.
- introduce activities designed to stimulate the learner's interest in sound e.g. musical instruments, sound effects, everyday noises (electric whisk, doorbell), feeling vibrations on your neck with his/her hand whilst singing or talking.
- practice locating sounds. Can the learner turn his/her head to the sound, reach out for it, explore the sound source?
- focus on listening by saying and using a sign for 'listen'.

Information

Further practical suggestions for teaching approaches for hearing, mobility and other aspects can be found in Bradley, H. and Snow, B. (1994) *Making Sense of the World: A Guide for Carers Working with People who have Combined Sensory and Learning Difficulties*. London: Sense.

The development of personal confidence and self-esteem is central to the entire framework. It is included in this chapter because learners with sensory impairments may miss the subtle clues of appreciation; a nod, a smile, an admiring tone of voice and, therefore, require specific support to develop in this area.

Personal development (confidence and self-esteem)

Some guidelines for enabling personal development

- Achievable objectives: challenging learners in small achievable steps raises self-esteem by experience of success.
- Structures/approaches to enable learners to take control: If a session structure is clear and repeated, learners are able to understand the options available and may learn to negotiate changes to the plan. Experiential approaches may be used to ensure the learner's forms of communication are 'heard'.
- Flexible practice: practitioners willing to listen to or observe the learner's choices and change the plan immediately to accommodate individual 'comment'.
- Positive feedback: the learner should receive a very clear message from practitioners that they are welcome, important, appreciated and that his/her contribution to the situation is valued highly. This may be achieved in many ways; body language, tone of voice, personal attention, quality of touch. Learners with sensory impairments may require much greater clarity and reinforcement to receive this message.

Craig's case

Craig is hearing impaired and blind. At first he exhibited aggressive challenging behaviours. Four triggers were identified: thirst, feeling insecure, needing the toilet, feeling ill. Learning programmes were introduced, based on Craig's preferred activities, to help Craig to communicate his needs appropriately. As he became familiar with the practitioners, structures and environment, he was able to take control of his learning appropriately, by taking people to the area of a favourite task or by choosing an object of reference.

Further comment relevant to the personal development segment is located in the Introduction, Chapter 2, Chapter 3 (Relationship building), Chapter 4 (Self-advocacy), Chapter 7 (Choice) and Chapter 10 (Enabling the learner to lead).

Chapter 12

The collaborative framework

'Diversity and complexity of needs indicate a coordinated inter-agency and inter-professional response'

(Evers *et al.* 1994).

In this chapter we review in brief the need for collaboration between services and outline the potential for extending and amending the framework to encompass different aspects of the life of the individual with profound and complex learning difficulties. The role of the framework in facilitating an individual learner focus across services is considered, in respect of its use as a linking device and in its potential for facilitating clearer communication and understanding between people involved directly in the life of the individual learner.

Why collaborate?

'Without inter-professional work ... the consequences are fragmentation of the field and isolated or disjointed action'

(Rawson 1994).

Individuals with profound and complex learning difficulties often come into contact with a range of people and services e.g. family, carers, friends, advocates, volunteers, professionals. There is a danger that the learner will encounter a fragmented and confusing array of people, environments and approaches to learning. Effective collaboration at all levels could reduce this difficulty and, therefore, benefit the learner.

Some benefits of collaboration are:

- the individual will receive a better service and may progress more quickly if learning objectives are practised consistently in different settings;
- those collaborating make use of each other's skills and training;

- there is joined up service;
- a shared knowledge about important details;
- reduced duplication of resources;
- shared problem solving;
- common ground between services with different cultures and philosophies;
- increased understanding of other services;
- stronger working relationships and good will.

Some barriers to effective collaboration are:

- language specific to a discipline which is not understood by others;
- separate funding;
- different philosophies and cultures;
- vested interests;
- lack of clear roles and responsibilities;
- status conflicts;
- lack of contact between services, not knowing who to contact;
- work overload;
- stereotyped assumptions about what each service can/does provide;
- lack of agreement about goals;
- feeling threatened about working with others.

Ways of overcoming barriers would be:

- focus on individual learner;
- staff training in interpersonal skills and understanding different perspectives;
- fostering an attitude which assumes that we all have something to contribute;
- sharing information and records within sensible, clear and agreed boundaries in relation to confidentiality;
- regular meetings, well run and organised to reduce unnecessary loss of time;
- strong informal networks;
- adopting strategies for building positive working relationships;
- contracting arrangements which specify requirements for collaboration.

> **Information**
>
> For further information on overcoming barriers to collaboration see Lacey, P. and Lomas, J. (1993) *Support Services and the Curriculum* (see References). For examples of good practice, refer to Appendix 2 of Leslie, I. (ed.) (1999) *Making Partnerships Work* (see References).

Using the framework in different settings

During the writing of this book, discussions with carers and colleagues from different professional backgrounds took place to consider the potential for extending and amending the framework to encompass different aspects of the life of the individual with profound and complex learning difficulties and to link with the areas of expertise of a range of providers. Further work is required to draw reliable conclusions. However, it is interesting to note the many areas of overlap and the very different ways in which these are described by people from varied professional backgrounds.

Figure 12.1 provides some practical examples and shows how the framework could be used as a basis for a common

> **Paul's case**
>
> Paul is a quiet man. He seems withdrawn at times, but quite suddenly becomes animated when something strikes him as interesting or funny. He has profound learning difficulties and visual impairment. As a result of Paul's individual planning, he was introduced to a range of new experiences, many of which took place outside of the home environment e.g. work experience (gardening), Indian restaurants, College, music therapy. However, he often became very distressed when it was time to go out. A range of strategies were devised to support Paul. It was established that he needed time to adjust to the idea of going out and that Paul needed to know and make contact with the person who was going with him. In addition, Paul began to use objects of reference. They were used to reinforce words and signs, so that he could understand where he was going. As well as home, each service was given a set of objects of reference for Paul to use. Over time, Paul was able to indicate his preferences using objects of reference e.g. he always smiled when handed the swimsuit and towel. He enjoyed swimming.

Individual learning need/choice e.g. from Person Centred Planning	Organisation/setting (examples)	Main area of framework (N.B. in practice most learning can be included in many framework areas)
Jill – learning to communicate her choice between two options by touching preference.	All settings e.g. home, college, work, therapy.	Foundation skill (Chapter 3)
Bob – learning new gardening skills (favourite activity).	• Careers – job in local park/ecology centre • Home – house plants or garden • College – environmental studies course	Science and technology (Chapter 5)
Shellan – using touch sensitive switch to operate equipment.	• Home – turn on kettle • Leisure – operating CD player at club • College/other – choosing by clicking on computer pictures	Science and technology (Chapter 5)
Lim – using money	• at the pub with advocate • in the college coffee shop • in the pinball and snooker machines at the club	Life skills (Chapter 7) and Basic study skills (Chapter 8)

Figure 12.1   Examples of linkages between the learner and the framework in different settings

ground between services in terms of thinking about and describing their work together.

If providers take a collaborative approach to working with people with profound and complex learning difficulties, one of the key areas of overlap will be the development of communication between the learner and other people. Sharing of critical knowledge is fundamental e.g. that when Kay looks down, it often means that she would like to go to the toilet. In addition, the process of relationship building will need to be undertaken by each person in each setting. Sharing reports of this process with each other may help to identify a starting point for developing relationships with new people which is meaningful for the learner.

Managers need to adopt a range of roles in order to facilitate collaboration. Joint strategic planning, resourcing and communication between services are key areas which are increasingly being demanded through legislative changes in Social Services and Health as well as Education. For the purposes of this book, we will focus on more operational considerations and consider some of the ways in which managers may be able to foster a culture of inter-agency collaboration.

Role of the manager in enabling collaboration

Information

The Department of Health has published a series of materials relating to collaboration between agencies, including a guide for practitioners in housing, health and social services: *Making Partnerships Work in Community Care* (1997).

Fostering inter-agency collaboration

- *shared aims*
  Members of organisations must be clear about aims and rationale in relation to collaborative work and ways in which they are expected to enact this in practice (refer to Chapter 1).
- *individual learner focus*
  The difficulties of blurring roles, dealing with power games and conflicts of interest require resolution in the face of clear commitment to the individual learner (see Chapter 1).
- *recruitment*
  Communication of the culture of an organisation begins at recruitment (refer to Chapter 1).
- *joint induction and training*
  Staff need time to reflect on the potential benefits and pitfalls of working collaboratively. They may require support to work through issues about roles and to understand and practise the interpersonal skills required to master inter-professional etiquette.
- *time for collaborating*
  Collaborating consumes time. People require time to be allowed for discussions. Managers need to provide this time.
- *Coordination and communication*
  A system or set of agreed practices is required to ensure

that carers and practitioners from different agencies are kept informed of relevant decisions.

- *Regular evaluations of collaborative work are required to guide change.*

Example feedback system

A survey of carers indicated that they appreciated face-to-face communication with College staff in preference to written communication. A feedback system was initiated involving a member of College staff being assigned to each home for liaison. Staff were given training in establishing contact with carers, managing conversations, providing relevant information using appropriate language etc. At minimum, the flow of information has improved and, in some cases, relationships have been established which result in carers feeling sufficiently comfortable to contact their link person if they are short staffed and 'need a hand' e.g. with supporting learners at a mealtime. This mix of formal and informal operating can form the basis for stronger relationships and extend communications beyond functional aspects (e.g. transport, timing) into more meaningful aspects (e.g. details about learner preferences and responses).

A key element of successful collaboration is to equip all staff with skills in a way which enables each of them to function as an agent of collaboration. It is then to provide appropriate support because it can be difficult and stressful, and to structure working patterns to allow time for collaboration to take place.

Allowing time for collaboration

- Encourage networking with learners present e.g. invite carers into session sometimes for the last half hour to sample learners' cooking or admire their art and computer work and to talk informally with the learner and the staff (refer to Chapter 2).
- Allow time between sessions for discussion between staff, 'phone calls to carers and others etc.
- Schedule open days/evenings.
- Provide flexibility within staffing arrangements so that front line staff can be released to attend relevant meetings e.g. for 'person centred planning' (McIntosh and Whittaker 2000).
- Allow management time for discussion with other

services regarding timetabling in accordance with the needs and preferences of each learner.

Freda's case

Freda attends a therapy-based day service. She goes horse riding and she attends drama therapy and physiotherapy. She would like to attend College so that she can build on some of the skills and personal development work achieved and work towards more inclusive opportunities. The College does not organise courses and expect the learner to 'fit in' to them. Instead the strengths, needs and preferences of each person are considered and groups and subjects built around them. A member of the College team visits the therapy centre and together they establish who should provide what and when, to suit Freda's needs and preferences. The College and Freda benefit from the insights offered by the therapy staff who already know Freda very well.

Collaboration is a highly complex task to undertake. It requires 'the political will and management resource support to enable professionals, users and carers to work together in times of change which require an approach of flexibility, cohesion and mutual understanding' (Leathard 1994). Not only is it a challenge to practitioners and managers, but also to the learners themselves. Griffiths (1994) raises the point that a learner cannot 'take on an adult role in working with the agencies who service him or her without learning how to do it.' Person centred planning involves bringing together the learner and the people who live, work or socialise directly with him or her, in order to '[support] each person to make a plan of their life, the help they need to do it and who will help them' (McIntosh and Whittaker 2000). This is an excellent example of the type of structured process required to facilitate collaboration and to enable the learner to take on an adult role in working with agencies. Following on from person centred planning, it may be helpful to conceptualise the implementation of the range of individual goals and activities by using and extending the framework (refer to Figure 12.1). In this way, the framework can be used to break down barriers to collaboration by forming the basis of a common language and way of thinking between learners, practitioners and managers.

References

Ackerman, D. and Mount, H. (1991) *Literacy For All*. London: David Fulton Publishers.

Aherne, P. *et al.* (1990) *Communication for All*. London: David Fulton Publishers.

Allen, C. and Mackay, H. (1996) *Creativity with People with Learning Disabilities: Practical Ideas With and Without Equipment*. Video Training Pack. 2nd edn. London: Orchard Hill College.

Allen, C. (2000) 'Education', in McIntosh, B. and Whittaker, A. (eds) *Unlocking the Future; Developing New Lifestyles with People who have Complex Disabilities*. London: King's Fund Publishing.

Bradley, H. (1991) *Assessing Communication Together*. Nottingham: APLD.

Bradley, H. and Snow, B. (1994) *Making Sense of the World: A Guide for Carers Working with People who have Combined Sensory and Learning Disabilities*. London: Sense.

Bradshaw, J. (1998) *The Role of Communication in Providing Quality Services for People with Learning Disabilities*. Handout for Planning for People presentation. Brighton: Pavilion Publishing.

Brennan, W. (1985) *Curriculum for Special Needs*. Milton Keynes: Open University Press.

Bruce, I.W. *et al.* (1991) *Blind and Partially Sighted Adults in Britain: The RNIB Survey*. Vol.1. London: HMSO.

Byers, R. (1998) 'Managing the Learning Environment', in Lacey, P. and Ouvry, C. (eds) *People with Profound and Multiple Learning Disabilities* 12, 117–29. London: David Fulton Publishers.

Campbell, M. *et al.* (1996) *Approaches to People with Profound and Complex Disabilities* 3, 106–39. Brighton: Pavilion Publishers.

Collis, M. and Lacey, P. (1996) *Interactive Approaches to Teaching: A Framework for INSET*. London: David Fulton Publishers.

Craft, A. (1999) *Creativity Across the Primary Curriculum: Framing and Developing Practice.* London: Routledge.

Deaf Blind Manual Alphabet. Sense. The National Deaf-Blind and Rubella Association (see Useful addresses section).

De Bono, E. (1995) *Serious Creativity.* London: Harper Collins.

Department of Health (1997) *Making Partnerships Work in Community Care.* London: Department of Health.

Department for Education (1995) *Key Stages 1 and 2 of the National Curriculum.* London: Department for Education.

Detheridge, T. and Detheridge M. (1997) *Literacy Through Symbols.* London: David Fulton Publishers.

Eales, J. (1991) 'An approach to health education for pupils with severe learning difficulties' in Scottish Health Education Group/Scottish Consultative Council on the Curriculum *Innovatory Practice and Severe Learning Difficulties*, 47. Edinburgh. Moray House Publications.

Equals (1999a) *Baseline Assessment and Curriculum Target Setting.* North Shields: Equals (see Useful addresses section).

Equals (1999b) *Moving On: Life Skills Book One.* North Shields: Equals.

Evers, H. *et al.* (1994) 'Inter-professional work with old and disabled people', in Leathard, A. (ed.) *Going Inter-Professional: Working together for Health and Welfare.* London: Routledge.

Farrell, P., *et al.* (1992) *EDY: Teaching People with Severe Learning Difficulties*, 2nd edn. Manchester University Press.

The Further Education Funding Council (1999) National Report from The Inspectorate. *National Awards for Students with Learning Difficulties:* FEFC.

FEU (1990) *Developing Self Advocacy Skills with People with Disabilities and Learning Difficulties.* London: FEU.

FEU (1992) *Learning for Life.* London: Further Education Unit/ Mencap.

Golding, R. and Goldsmith, L. (1986) *The Caring Person's Guide to Handling the Severely Multiply Handicapped.* Hants and London: Macmillan Education.

Griffiths, M. (1994) *Transition to Adulthood.* London: David Fulton Publishers.

Griffiths, M. and Tennyson, C. (1997) *The Extended Curriculum.* London: David Fulton Publishers.

Gunstone, M. (1993) *You And Me Whole Body Movement.* You and Me Publications.

Hewett, D. and Nind, M. (eds) (1998) *Interaction In Action: Reflections on the use of Intensive Interaction.* London: David Fulton Publishers.

Hogg, J. (1998) 'Competence and quality in the lives of people with profound and multiple learning disabilities: some recent research', in *Tizard Learning Disability Review* **3**, 1.

Hurst, K.W. *et al.* (1995) *Nutrition by Design*. New Possibilities NHS Trust.

Hutchinson, M. (2001) *Discovery, Exploration and Problem-solving for People with Profound and Multiple Learning Difficulties*. Oxford: Winslow.

Johnson, G. and Scholes, K. (1997) *Exploring Corporate Strategy*, 4th edn. Hertfordshire: Prentice Hall.

Knight, T. (2000) 'Fundamental role of creativity', *Times Educational Supplement*. Curriculum special: Music and the Arts.

Knill, M. and Knill, C. (1986) *Activity Programmes for Body Awareness, Contact and Communication*. Cambridge: LDA.

Lacey, P. and Lomas, J. (1993) *Support Services and the Curriculum: A Practical Guide*. London: David Fulton Publishers.

Leathard, A. (1994) *Going Inter-Professional: Working Together for Health and Welfare*. London: Routledge.

Leslie, I. (ed.) (1999) *Making Partnerships Work: for Rehabilitation and Employment*. Richmond Fellowship Workschemes.

Marvin, C. (1998) 'Teaching and learning for children with profound and multiple learning difficulties', in Lacey, P. and Ouvry, C. (eds) *People with Profound and Multiple Learning Disabilities* **10**, 117–29. London: David Fulton Publishers.

McConkey, R. (1994) *Innovations in Educating Communities about Disabilities*. Lancashire: Lisieux Hall Publications.

McConkey, R. (1998) 'Community integration and ordinary lifestyles', in Lacey, P. and Ouvry, C. (eds) *People with Profound and Multiple Learning Disabilities: A Collaborative Approach to Meeting Complex Needs*. London: David Fulton Publishers.

McGee, J.J. *et al.* (1987) *Gentle Teaching: A Nonaversive Approach to Helping Persons with Mental Retardation*. New York: Human Sciences Press.

McInnes, J. and Treffry, J. (1982) *Deaf-blind Infants and Children. A Developmental Guide*. Milton Keynes: OUP.

McIntosh, B. (1999) 'Day opportunities for the future', Paper presented at *Day Options for People with Learning Disabilities*, Pavilion Publishing Conference, London.

McIntosh, B. and Whittaker, A. (2000) *Unlocking the Future: Developing New Lifestyles with People who have Complex Disabilities*. London: King's Fund Publishing.

McLeod, W.T. (1995) *The New Collins Concise Dictionary*. London: Guild Publishing.

Merriam-Webster (2000) Online Dictionary. www.m-w.com/dictionary.htm

Miller, J. (1998) *People with Profound and Multiple Learning Disabilities*. London: David Fulton Publishers.

Nind, M. and Hewett, D. (1994) *Access to Communication: Developing the Basics of Communication in People with Severe Learning Difficulties through Intensive Interaction*. London: David Fulton Publishers.

Ockleford, A. (1994) *Objects of Reference: Promoting Communication Skills and Development in Visually Impaired Children who have other Disabilities*. London: Royal National Institute for the Blind.

Orchard Hill College (1999) *Prospectus*. Orchard Hill College.

Park, K. (1998) *Objects of Reference*. RNIB Focus newsletter 25. London: Royal National Institute for the Blind.

Pick, C. (1993) *RNIB Certificate in Multiple Disability: Visual Function Assessments*. London: Royal National Institute for the Blind.

Pointer, B. (1993) *Activities for People with a Multiple Disability*. London: The Spastics Society.

Rawson, D. (1994) 'Models of inter-professional work' in Leathard, A. *Going Inter-professional: Working Together for Health and Welfare*. London: Routledge.

Rodbroe, I. and Hayes, T. (1997) *Communication through Active Music*. Video and booklet. London: Royal National Institute for the Deaf.

Rodgers, J. (1998) 'Whatever's on her plate: food in the lives of people with learning disabilities', *British Journal of Learning Disabilities* **26**, 13–16. British Institute of Learning Disabilities Publications.

Royal National Institute for the Blind (1992) *Looking for Eye Problems in People with Learning Difficulties*. London: Royal National Institute for the Blind.

Royal National Institute for the Blind (1995) *How to Guide a Blind Person*, 2nd edn. London: Royal National Institute for the Blind.

Royal National Institute for the Blind (1996) *Looking for Hearing Problems in People with Learning Difficulties*. London: Royal National Institute for the Blind.

Royal National Institute for the Blind (1998) *Access to Eyecare for Adults with Learning Difficulties*. London: Royal National Institute for the Blind.

Samuel, J. and Maggs, J. (1998) 'Introducing Intensive Interaction for people with profound learning disabilities in small staffed houses in the community', in Hewett, D. and Nind, M. (eds) *Interaction in Action: Reflections on the Use of Intensive Interaction*. London: David Fulton Publishers.

Sanderson, H. *et al*. (1991) *Aromatherapy and Massage for People with Learning Difficulties*. Birmingham: Hands on Publishing and Training.

Sanderson, H. (1995) 'Self-advocacy and inclusion: Supporting people with profound and multiple disabilities', in Philpot, T. and Ward, L. (eds.) *Value and Visions*. Oxford: Butterworth Heinemann Publishers.

Sebba, J. *et al.* (1993) *Redefining the Whole Curriculum for People with Learning Difficulties*. London: David Fulton Publishers.

Simons, K. (1999) *A Place at the Table? Involving People with Learning Difficulties in Purchasing and Commissioning Services*. Plymouth: British Institute of Learning Disabilities Publications.

Standard Manual Alphabet. Royal National Institute for the Deaf (see Useful addresses section).

Sutcliffe, J. (1990) *Adults with Learning Difficulties: Education for Choice and Empowerment*. Leicester: N.I.A.C.E.

Tilstone, C. and Barry, C. (1998) ' Advocacy and empowerment: what does it mean for pupils and people with PMLD?', in Lacey, P. and Ouvry, C. (eds) *People with Profound and Multiple Learning Difficulties: A Collaborative Approach to Meeting Complex Needs.* **15**, 180. London: David Fulton Publishers.

Ware, J. (1996) *Creating a Responsive Environment*. London: David Fulton Publishers.

Warren, D. (1994) *Blindness and Children: An Individual Differences Approach*. Cambridge: Cambridge University Press.

Wertheimer, A. (1996a) *Getting Ready for Work*. London: National Bureau for Students with Disabilities.

Wertheimer, A. (1996b) *Changing Days: Developing New Day Opportunities with People Who Have Learning Difficulties*. London: King's Fund Publishing.

Wyatt, J. and Sherratt, B. (1996) *A Structured Approach to School and Staff Development*. Occasional Paper, Series 4, No 1. The Grant Maintained Schools Centre.

Useful addresses

ALL (Accreditation for life and living skills) is merging with OCR (Oxford, Cambridge and RSA). Progress House, Westwood Way, Coventry CV4 8JQ. Tel: 02476 470033.

Award Scheme Development and Accreditation Network (ASDAN). Tel: 0117 946 6228. E-Mail: Asdan@uwe.ac.uk

Equals (Entitlement and quality education for pupils with severe learning difficulties). P.O. Box 107, North Shields, Tyne and Wear NE30 2YG. Tel: 0191 272 8600.

Makaton Vocabulary Development Project, 31 Firwood Drive, Camberley, Surrey GU15 3QD.

MENCAP National Office, 123 Golden Lane, London EC1Y 0RT. Tel: 020 7454 0454.

National Open College Network, Runnymede Centre, Chertsey Road, Addlestone, Surrey KT15 2EP. Tel: 01932 569894.

PLANET (Play Leisure Advice Network) Cambridge House, Cambridge Grove, London W6 0LE. Tel: 020 8741 4119.

Royal National Institute for the Blind (RNIB) information service. 224, Great Portland Street, London W1N 6AA. Tel: 020 7388 1266.

Royal National Institute the Deaf (RNID), 19-21 Featherstone Street, London EC1Y 8SL. Tel: 020 7296 8000. (Suppliers of Standard Manual Alphabet.)

SENSE. The National Deaf-Blind and Rubella Association, 11–13 Clifton Terrace, Finsbury Park, London N4 3SR. Tel: 020 7272 7774. (Suppliers of Deaf Blind Manual Alphabet.)

The Signalong Group, 129 Rochester Road, Burham, Rochester, Kent ME1 3SG.

Skill (National Bureau for students with disabilities) information service. Chapter House, 18–20 Crucifix Lane, London SE1 3JW. Tel: 0207 450 0620.

Symwrite 2000: overlays and related software can be ordered through SEMERC. Tel: 0161 8272887.

Widgit Software Ltd, 102 Radford Road, Leamington Spa CV31 1LF. Tel: 01926 885303. Email: Literacy@widgit.com for 'Writing with Symbols' software PCS (Picture Communication Symbols), see Chapter 8.

Winslow. Tel: 01869 244 644 for Colour Cards, in Chapter 8.

You and Me Yoga, Salked Cottage, Priest Hutton, Carnforth, Lancashire LA6 1JP. Tel/Fax: 01524782103. Email: maria@youand meyoga.com Www.youandmeyoga.com for vocational training programmes and materials, see Chapter 7.

Index